INTERNATIONAL DEVELOPMENT IN FOCUS

Fostering Human Capital in the Gulf Cooperation Council Countries

SAMEH EL-SAHARTY, IGOR KHEYFETS, CHRISTOPHER H. HERBST, AND MOHAMED IHSAN AJWAD

© 2020 International Bank for Reconstruction and Development / The World Bank
1818 H Street NW, Washington, DC 20433
Telephone: 202-473-1000; Internet: www.worldbank.org

Some rights reserved

1 2 3 4 23 22 21 20

Books in this series are published to communicate the results of Bank research, analysis, and operational experience with the least possible delay. The extent of language editing varies from book to book.

This work is a product of the staff of The World Bank with external contributions. The findings, interpretations, and conclusions expressed in this work do not necessarily reflect the views of The World Bank, its Board of Executive Directors, or the governments they represent. The World Bank does not guarantee the accuracy of the data included in this work. The boundaries, colors, denominations, and other information shown on any map in this work do not imply any judgment on the part of The World Bank concerning the legal status of any territory or the endorsement or acceptance of such boundaries.

Nothing herein shall constitute or be considered to be a limitation upon or waiver of the privileges and immunities of The World Bank, all of which are specifically reserved.

Rights and Permissions

This work is available under the Creative Commons Attribution 3.0 IGO license (CC BY 3.0 IGO) http://creativecommons.org/licenses/by/3.0/igo. Under the Creative Commons Attribution license, you are free to copy, distribute, transmit, and adapt this work, including for commercial purposes, under the following conditions:

Attribution—Please cite the work as follows: El-Saharty, Sameh, Igor Kheyfets, Christopher H. Herbst, and Mohamed Ihsan Ajwad. 2020. *Fostering Human Capital in the Gulf Cooperation Council Countries*. International Development in Focus. Washington, DC: World Bank. doi:10.1596/978-1-4648-1582-9. License: Creative Commons Attribution CC BY 3.0 IGO

Translations—If you create a translation of this work, please add the following disclaimer along with the attribution: *This translation was not created by The World Bank and should not be considered an official World Bank translation. The World Bank shall not be liable for any content or error in this translation.*

Adaptations—If you create an adaptation of this work, please add the following disclaimer along with the attribution: *This is an adaptation of an original work by The World Bank. Views and opinions expressed in the adaptation are the sole responsibility of the author or authors of the adaptation and are not endorsed by The World Bank.*

Third-party content—The World Bank does not necessarily own each component of the content contained within the work. The World Bank therefore does not warrant that the use of any third-party-owned individual component or part contained in the work will not infringe on the rights of those third parties. The risk of claims resulting from such infringement rests solely with you. If you wish to re-use a component of the work, it is your responsibility to determine whether permission is needed for that re-use and to obtain permission from the copyright owner. Examples of components can include, but are not limited to, tables, figures, or images.

All queries on rights and licenses should be addressed to World Bank Publications, The World Bank Group, 1818 H Street NW, Washington, DC 20433, USA; e-mail: pubrights@worldbank.org.

ISBN: 978-1-4648-1582-9
DOI: 10.1596/978-1-4648-1582-9

Cover photos: Flags, © Dana.S / Shutterstock.com; children (left side), © ZouZou / Shutterstock.com; women students (right side) © Dean Drobot / Shutterstock.com. All photos used with permission; further permission required for reuse.
Cover design: Debra Naylor / Naylor Design Inc.

Contents

Foreword vii
Acknowledgments ix
About the Authors xi
Abbreviations xiii

Overview 1
  Notes 4
  References 4

CHAPTER 1 The Human Capital Project 5
  Human capital and economic growth 5
  The human capital project: A measure of
    potential productivity 6
  HCI scores in the GCC countries 6
  Accelerating human capital formation: A lifelong approach 9
  Human capital and COVID-19 10
  Notes 11
  References 11

CHAPTER 2 Four Main Challenges in Human Capital Formation 13
  Poor learning outcomes 13
  Mismatch between education outcomes and labor
    market needs 17
  Relatively high adult mortality and morbidity 20
  A unique labor market 22
  Notes 25
  References 25

**CHAPTER 3 Four Strategies for Accelerating Human
Capital Formation** 27
  Investing in high-quality early childhood development 27
  Preparing youth for the future 30
  Enabling greater adult labor force participation 32
  Creating an enabling environment for human
    capital formation 35
  Note 37
  References 37

CHAPTER 4	**The GCC Countries' Responses to COVID-19** **39**
	Background 39
	Implications for human capital 41
	Measures taken by the GCC countries 44
	Possible additional measures 49
	Public health considerations for reopening an economy 51
	Final thoughts 55
	Notes 55
	References 57
CHAPTER 5	**Conclusion** **59**
APPENDIX A	**Government Visions for Accelerating Human Capital Formation** **61**
APPENDIX B	**GCC Country Profiles** **69**

Boxes

2.1 Recent Programme for International Student Assessment results   15
3.1 Prioritizing early childhood education in the United Arab Emirates   29

Figures

1.1 Human Capital Index: International benchmarking, 2018   8
1.2 Human Capital Index, by income group, 2018   8
1.3 A lifelong approach to human capital: Realizing the full potential of a productive population   10
2.1 TIMSS grade 4 mathematics performance and GDP per capita, 2015   14
2.2 Percentage of students in the Gulf Cooperation Council countries reaching the "low" international benchmark in TIMSS 2015 and PIRLS 2016, by subject   14
2.3 Learning-adjusted years of school in Gulf Cooperation Council countries, by gender, 2018   15
2.4 TIMSS grade 4 mathematics performance gaps in the Gulf Cooperation Council countries, 2015   16
2.5 Four tensions holding back education systems in the Gulf Cooperation Council countries   18
2.6 Gulf Cooperation Council countries stuck in a credentialist equilibrium   18
2.7 Percentage of grade 8 students asked to memorize science facts and principles for every lesson or almost every lesson, 2015   19
2.8 Burden of disease attributable to six leading risk factors in the Gulf Cooperation Council countries, 2017   21
2.9 Percentage of GDP spent on health in OECD and GCC member states   22
2.10 Share of foreign nationals in the total population, Gulf Cooperation Council countries, circa 2016   23
2.11 Public sector employment in the Gulf Cooperation Council countries   23
2.12 Female labor force participation versus income in the Gulf Cooperation Council countries   24
3.1 Yielding high returns with investment in the early years   28
3.2 Preprimary education gross enrollment rates in Gulf Cooperation Council and high-income countries, 1976, 1996, and 2016   29
4.1 Trend of COVID-19 cases in the Gulf Cooperation Council countries, total of confirmed cases (as of June 8, 2020)   40

Tables

1.1 Learning-adjusted years of school in the Gulf Cooperation Council countries, 2018   7
1.2 Human Capital Index in the Gulf Cooperation Council countries, 2018   7
2.1 Percentage of grade 4 students whose principals report that teacher absenteeism or tardiness is a serious or moderate problem, 2015   17
2.2 Life expectancy, 2016, and adult mortality and disability-adjusted life years, 2017, in the GCC countries   20
2.3 Percentage of total deaths and DALYs caused by NCDs and TIs   20
4.1 Status of COVID-19 in the Gulf Cooperation Council countries   40
4.2 Global Health Security Index and rank of the GCC countries   42

Foreword

Human capital plays a critical role in the economic development of the countries of the Gulf Cooperation Council (GCC). Investing in people promotes greater equity and economic growth, with broad implications for the welfare and prosperity of people as well as of countries. Most GCC countries have a strong focus on human development in their development strategies and have allocated significant shares of their budgets to human capital, but they could do more to improve the effectiveness of these investments.

Economic transformation is a long-term endeavor, requiring steadfast, coordinated implementation. The GCC governments have demonstrated their strong political will for this transformation by being among the first to join the World Bank's Human Capital Project. This project is a global effort to improve investments in people through contributions to three areas—knowledge, skills, and health—which are quantified by the Human Capital Index (HCI). The HCI measures the contribution of health and education to the productivity of the next generation of workers. More specifically, it reflects the human capital a child born today can expect to accumulate by age 18, given the risks to health and education in the country in which the child lives. Although the GCC countries have recognized the importance of human capital, they could do more. Currently, the GCC countries rank higher on the HCI than the average of the Middle East and North Africa region as a whole, but lower than their peers in other regions with similar levels of per capita income. This relative ranking indicates that poor learning outcomes, inadequate development of skills, and high rates of health problems are slowing human capital formation and hampering moves toward sustainable and equitable growth. To mitigate this trend, the GCC countries should increase their human capital by accelerating improvements in learning, skills, and health outcomes for their citizens.

After reviewing the main challenges for human capital formation in the GCC countries in education, health, and labor markets, and then encapsulating the six governments' own plans in this area, this report highlights four main strategies that the GCC countries can pursue to accelerate human capital formation: (1) invest in high-quality early childhood development, (2) prepare youth for the future, (3) enable greater participation in the labor force of the adult population, and (4) create an enabling environment for human capital formation.

While job creation is the overarching goal of the broader drive for diversification, sustainable employment will require a vibrant and robust private sector that can compete with the public sector. This shift will entail the promotion of a labor market that allows for flexibility, skill-building, and reasonable compensation. Moreover, given the youth bulge in the GCC countries, policies to target job creation for youth, as well as for women, are high priorities.

Investments in human capital have become increasingly important as the nature of work is evolving in response to rapid technological changes. How the GCC countries address these challenges—especially in light of the COVID-19 pandemic, which struck as this document was being finalized—will shape their future.

Issam Abousleiman
Regional Director
GCC Country Department
The World Bank

Keiko Miwa
Regional Director
Human Development
The World Bank

Acknowledgments

This report was prepared by a World Bank team led by Sameh El-Saharty, program leader for Human Development, the Gulf Cooperation Council (GCC) Department, and composed of Igor Kheyfets, senior education economist; Christopher H. Herbst, senior health specialist; and Mohamed Ihsan Ajwad, senior economist, social protection and jobs. Major contributions to chapter 4 were provided by David Wilson, program director, Health, Nutrition and Population Global Practice; Johannes Koettl, senior economist, Carole Chartouni, senior social protection specialist, and Ahmet Fatih Ortakaya, senior social protection specialist, Social Protection and Jobs Practice Group; and Laura Gregory, senior education specialist, Education Global Practice Group. The report was prepared under the guidance of Issam Abousleiman, regional director for the GCC country department; Keiko Miwa, regional director for Human Capital, Middle East and North Africa; and Sona Varma, lead economist.

The report was peer-reviewed by Safaa El-Tayeb El-Kogali, then education practice manager, Middle East and North Africa; Andreas Blom, education practice manager, Middle East and North Africa; Kamel Braham, program leader for Human Development, Mashreq Countries Department; and Fernando Xavier Montenegro Torres, senior health economist, Middle East and North Africa.

The authors benefited from comments received from Sahar Hussein, economist, and Daniel Lederman, lead economist, Social Protection and Jobs; Paul Moreno-Lopez, program leader for Economics and Finance, GCC Department; Jamal Al-Kibbi, resident representative, United Arab Emirates; Ghassan Al-Khoja, resident representative, Kuwait; and Alexandra Pugachevsky, country program coordinator.

Background research was provided by Aviva Chengcheng Liu, Human Development consultant, and by Jonathan Aspin, Human Development consultant and editor. Editing services were provided by Jee Yoon Lee, editor.

About the Authors

Mohamed Ihsan Ajwad is a senior economist in the Social Protection and Jobs Global Practice at the World Bank in Washington, DC. He has managed diverse multisectoral teams that successfully delivered development policy operations, investment projects, technical assistance, reimbursable advisory services, and analytical services. He has worked on high-, middle-, and low-income countries in Africa, Europe and Central Asia, Latin America, the Middle East and North Africa, and South Asia. Notably, Ihsan led or co-led the work on monitoring the social impacts of the Great Recession in Europe and Central Asia; the Jobs Development Policy Operation in Kosovo; the Skills and Jobs Investment Project Financing in Kazakhstan; and several jobs diagnostics and strategies, including in Azerbaijan, Georgia, Kuwait, Saudi Arabia, and Tajikistan. He earned his doctorate in economics at the University of Illinois at Urbana-Champaign.

Sameh El-Saharty is the program leader for Human Development responsible for the World Bank's advisory services in health, education, social protection, and jobs in the Gulf Cooperation Council (GCC) countries. Since joining the World Bank in 1998, he has been responsible for leading policy dialog and strategy development as well as preparing and managing programs and projects in more than 25 countries in Africa, Asia, and the Middle East, as well as in the United States. His work has recently focused on human capital formation in the GCC countries, notably on health, education, and skills development. Previously, his work was concentrated on health reform, finance, service delivery, and implementation science. Before joining the World Bank, he held several positions with the World Health Organization, the United States Agency for International Development, the United Nations Population Fund, Harvard University, and Pathfinder International. He also was an assistant professor at Georgetown University. He has authored more than 30 publications, including journal articles, books, book chapters, analytical reports, and policy briefs. He is a medical doctor with a master's degree in international health policy and management from Harvard University.

Christopher H. Herbst is a senior health specialist in the World Bank's Health, Nutrition and Population Global Practice. He is based in Saudi Arabia, where he is coordinating the World Bank's engagement in the health sector, providing support in the areas of noncommunicable diseases, health financing, human resources for health, and pharmaceutical systems, among other areas. Throughout his career at the World Bank, Christopher has worked in more than 25 low-, middle-, and high-income countries in Africa, Asia, and the Middle East. His research and publications focus on health systems strengthening and health workforce issues. He obtained undergraduate, graduate, and postgraduate degrees from King's College London, the London School of Economics and Political Science, and Lancaster University, respectively.

Igor Kheyfets is a senior economist in the World Bank's Education Global Practice, focusing on the Middle East and North Africa region. Since joining the World Bank in 2008, he has worked on issues including education finance, efficiency of resource utilization, use of data and analysis for policy making, and the links between graduates' skills and the labor market. He has written working papers and analytical reports on these topics, including more than a dozen public expenditure reviews in education, and has led operational engagements in Eastern Europe, Central Asia, and the Middle East and North Africa. He is a co-founder of the World Bank's BOOST initiative for public expenditure analysis and holds a master's degree in public policy from Georgetown University.

Abbreviations

DALYs	disability-adjusted life years
ECD	early childhood development
edtech	education technology
GCC	Gulf Cooperation Council
GDP	gross domestic product
GHSI	Global Health Security Index
HCI	Human Capital Index
IEA	International Association for the Evaluation of Educational Achievement
IHME	Institute for Health Metrics and Evaluation
LAYS	learning-adjusted years of school
MENA	Middle East and North Africa
MOE	Ministry of Education
MOH	Ministry of Health
MOPH	Ministry of Public Health
NCDs	noncommunicable diseases
OECD	Organisation for Economic Co-operation and Development
PIRLS	Progress in International Reading Literacy Study
PISA	Programme for International Student Assessment
TIMSS	Trends in Mathematics and Science Study
TIs	transport injuries
UNESCO	United Nations Educational, Scientific, and Cultural Organization
WHO	World Health Organization

All dollar amounts are US dollars unless otherwise indicated.

Overview

Human capital formation is vital for the countries of the Gulf Cooperation Council (GCC). Expanding human capital has implications not only for human development and employment but also for the long-term sustainability of a diversified, knowledge-based, and private sector–driven economic growth model. The GCC countries have been investing in improving the knowledge, skills, and health of their populations, and joined the World Bank's Human Capital Project launched in 2018. These countries' scores on the Human Capital Index (HCI) are, however, lower than those of countries at comparable levels of income, underlining the need to increase the returns on human capital investment in the region and the associated challenges of doing so.

These challenges include poor learning outcomes of young children in basic levels of proficiency, a mismatch between education and the skills needed in the labor market, relatively high rates of adult mortality and morbidity, and a unique labor market in which there is a high wage differential between public and private sector jobs. Strategies to overcome these issues include investing in high-quality early childhood development, preparing youth for the job market, enabling greater adult labor force participation, and creating an environment for human capital to thrive.

What is "human capital"? The term refers to the knowledge, skills, and health that people accumulate over their lifetimes. By investing in human capital, countries in the GCC can enable people to maximize their potential as productive members of society. The World Bank's HCI measures (1) survival, indicating a child's likelihood of surviving to age 5; (2) schooling, measuring the learning-adjusted years of school, which combine the *quantity* of education a child can expect to have had by age 18 with the *quality* of education (given that children in some countries learn far less than children in others over a similar period); and (3) health, reflecting the rate of stunted growth of children under age 5, and the adult survival rate, or the proportion of 15-year-olds who will survive until age 60.

The HCI ranges between 0 and 1. A score of 1 would mean that a country has full health and full education. Full health means there is no stunting and there is a 100 percent adult survival rate between ages 15 and 60. Full education means that there are 14 years of high-quality schooling by age 18. A score of 0.70 would indicate that the future productivity of a child born today falls 30 percent below the maximum health and education levels of the index.

Although the GCC countries' HCI scores vary, the scores are relatively low, ranging from 0.58 to 0.67, indicating that a child born today in a GCC country will only attain between 58 percent and 67 percent of his or her full health, learning, and potential productivity. Bahrain has the highest HCI score, at 0.67, ranking 47th in the world, followed by the United Arab Emirates (0.66, 49th), Oman (0.62, 54th), Qatar (0.61, 60th), Saudi Arabia (0.58, 73rd), and Kuwait (0.58, 77th).

HCI scores in the GCC countries are higher than the scores of their regional peers but lower than their economic peers' scores. Scores for human capital in the GCC countries rank at the top in the Middle East and North Africa (MENA) region and are higher than the MENA average of 0.56. Over the past decade, the GCC countries have in fact been doing better than other countries in the region, overtaking Jordan, Lebanon, and Tunisia in international standardized reading and mathematics tests. However, the GCC countries do not compare favorably with countries such as Germany, the Republic of Korea, or Singapore, which have similar income levels but significantly higher HCI scores. The scores in the GCC countries are similar to those in less wealthy nations, such as Mexico, Thailand, and Turkey.

This report outlines the four main challenges that hinder the development of human capital in the GCC countries:

- *Low levels of basic proficiency among schoolchildren.* Despite substantial public investment in education, all six GCC member countries score lower than other high-income countries on international student assessments. Moreover, although school enrollment rates are high, when adjusted for the quality of education that children receive, the *effective* educational attainment in the GCC countries is far lower. Also, substantial gender gaps in learning between girls and boys arise, with boys consistently *under*performing.
- *Mismatch between education and the labor market.* The skills taught in school do not adequately prepare students with the skills needed for employment.
- *The relatively high rate of adult mortality and morbidity due to noncommunicable diseases.* In 2016, average life expectancy at birth in the GCC countries was about 76 years—relatively high compared with Organisation for Economic Co-operation and Development countries. Yet mortality due to noncommunicable diseases is 71.5 percent, which is very high.
- *The unique labor market.* Wages in the public sector are more generous than in the private sector (where most new jobs need to be created), and the extension of government employment to nationals is almost guaranteed.

Four main strategies are suggested to help overcome these challenges and accelerate human capital formation:

- *Investing in high-quality early childhood development.* Investing in the early years of development would allow the GCC countries to improve the lifelong productivity of their people. Studies have shown that an effective way to address low basic proficiency among schoolchildren is to invest in early childhood education. A greater return on learning outcomes and lifelong productivity can be achieved when investments are made in the first six years of a child's development. During this period, the building blocks of the brain are formed, and the child's environment stimulates brain development.
- *Preparing youth for the future.* Improving learning outcomes, responding to labor market needs, and reducing health risk factors are all important for preparing youth for the future.

- *Enabling greater labor force participation by the adult population.* Adult labor force participation growth can be achieved by promoting lifelong learning, improving conditions for female labor force participation, providing retraining or upskilling for unemployed or underemployed adults, and improving health conditions to reduce adult mortality and morbidity.
- *Creating an enabling environment for human capital formation.* An environment that emphasizes productive human capital development will enable the GCC countries to increase value for money in public spending on education and health, to move toward a multisectoral approach to human capital, and to foster shared social norms and political interests that will lead to greater productivity and prosperity.

These strategies are based on good practices and evidence from implementation in other countries and feature, in part, some of the six countries' plans for developing their workforces, including their national "Visions" that have been crafted over the past decade or so.

Implementation of these strategies will require both a whole-of-government approach that will coordinate various sectoral inputs and ensure continuity across political cycles, and an alignment of social and political interests using public-awareness campaigns to change norms and behaviors to ensure understanding and support of people across sectors and communities.

When this report was being finalized, the COVID-19 disease, declared by the World Health Organization a global pandemic on March 11, 2020, had touched 188 countries and territories with more than 7 million infections and more than 403,000 deaths as of June 8.[1] Many governments worldwide adopted increasingly stringent health measures, such as lockdowns, alongside unprecedented economic measures. Children missed schooling, and the general population avoided accessing health care facilities. This unprecedented global pandemic puts the human capital gains made in any country over the years at significant risk.

With COVID-19, the need to accelerate and improve the investment in human capital has never been greater. Once the pandemic has run its course and the GCC countries return to what may well be a "new normal," these countries can, by implementing this report's recommended strategies for developing human capital, achieve diversified and sustainable growth that does not depend on hydrocarbons. The GCC countries could consider combining strategies to develop a dynamic private sector–led model of economic growth. At the moment, potential productivity gains are lost because of low female labor force participation rates and a skills mismatch. Policies geared toward improving the employability of women, while also addressing skills gaps through upskilling or reskilling, and aligning education and training systems with labor market demands, would improve productivity and economic growth in the GCC countries.[2] Moreover, developing a dynamic private sector by enhancing the business environment would help spur the creation of high-quality, productive jobs. Public sector wage reform could also be considered to help reduce distortions in the labor market that arise from high public wages.

In sum, the COVID-19 crisis underscores the urgency of enhancing human capital investment. In the GCC countries, both demand- and supply-side strategies for private sector development are critical for achieving productivity gains and building the foundations for a diversified and sustainable growth model. The GCC countries are ready to address the challenges and make their human capital central to the achievement of their growth strategies.

NOTES

1. "COVID-19 Dashboard by the Center for Systems Science and Engineering (CSSE) at Johns Hopkins University (JHU)," consulted June 8, 2020 (https://coronavirus.jhu.edu/map.html).
2. Constant (2016) finds that raising female employment to country-specific male levels in Denmark, the Arab Republic of Egypt, Japan, and the United Arab Emirates could increase gross domestic product by 4 percent, 56 percent, 15 percent, and 19 percent, respectively, by 2020.

REFERENCES

Constant, Samantha M. 2016. *Paving the Way for Women's Economic Inclusion in the Gulf Cooperation Council: Main Report (GCC)*. GCC Engagement Note. Washington, DC: World Bank.

World Bank. 2018. "Human Capital Project." https://www.worldbank.org/en/publication/human-capital.

1 The Human Capital Project

This report describes the World Bank's Human Capital Project (World Bank 2018) and presents the Human Capital Index (HCI) score for the Gulf Cooperation Council (GCC) countries relative to comparable countries. The report provides a summary of the four main challenges facing the formation of human capital in the GCC countries and suggests four key strategies for accelerating human capital formation to achieve economic diversification and sustainability. Appendix A outlines the salient features of the six governments' national "Visions."

HUMAN CAPITAL AND ECONOMIC GROWTH

Economic growth depends on human capital, physical capital, and factors affecting the productivity of both. Human capital consists of the knowledge, skills, and health that people accumulate over their lives to make them more productive. When governments make investments in human capital, they equip the workforce with the skills necessary to better utilize physical capital. Countries that have invested consistently over time to improve their human capital have observed tremendous gains. These countries include Finland, Ireland, the Republic of Korea, and Singapore. Studies have shown that the quality of education (learning) correlates strongly with economic growth; that psychosocial stimulation in early childhood years can raise adult income by up to 25 percent; and that one additional year of schooling raises an individual's earnings by 8 percent to 10 percent (Gertler and others 2014; Hanushek and Woessmann 2015). A study of the wealth of nations finds that human capital, measured as the value of earnings over an individual's lifetime, was the most important component of wealth globally compared with the other components, such as produced capital, natural wealth, and net financial assets. In high-income countries, the share of human capital wealth is about 66 percent of their total wealth, but only some 41 percent in low-income countries. In the GCC countries, the share of human capital in total wealth ranges from 24 percent in Kuwait to 58 percent in Bahrain (Lange, Wodon, and Carey 2018).

Investments in human capital have become increasingly important as the nature of work has evolved in response to rapid technological change. By one estimate, two-thirds of all jobs in the developing world are susceptible to automation (World Bank 2016). In addition, labor markets are demanding workers with higher-order cognitive, socioemotional, and behavioral skills (World Bank 2019b). Such automation is reshaping many aspects of work, shifting the demand for skills from narrow, job-specific, routine manual skills to advanced cognitive and sociobehavioral skills (Cunningham and Villaseñor 2016; Deming 2017; Hanushek and others 2017; Krueger and Kumar 2004). Skills associated with "adaptability" are increasingly in demand. Critically, this combination of specific cognitive skills (critical thinking and problem solving) and sociobehavioral skills (creativity and curiosity) is transferable across jobs.

THE HUMAN CAPITAL PROJECT: A MEASURE OF POTENTIAL PRODUCTIVITY

To reinforce the case for investing in people, the World Bank's Human Capital Project includes an index that captures the amount of capital (in knowledge, skills, and health) that a child born today could expect to attain by age 18.

The HCI has three components: (1) survival, indicating a child's likelihood of surviving to age 5; (2) learning, measuring the learning-adjusted years of school, which combines the quantity of education a child can expect to have had by age 18 with the quality of that education (given that children in some countries learn far less than children in others over a similar period); and (3) health, reflecting the rate of stunted children under age 5 and the adult survival rate, or the proportion of 15-year-olds who will survive until age 60.

The components of the index are combined to reflect their contributions to worker productivity. The index scale ranges between 0 and 1, and measures the following three components: survival, learning, and health. A score of 1 would mean that a country has full health and full education and that children will survive to age 5. Full health means that there is no stunting, and there is a 100 percent adult survival rate between ages 15 and 60. Full education entails 14 years of high-quality schooling by age 18. A score of 0.70 would indicate that the future productivity of a child born today is 30 percent below the maximum health and education levels of the index (World Bank 2018).

HCI SCORES IN THE GCC COUNTRIES

The GCC countries vary significantly across the HCI components:

Survival to age 5. As a result of the tremendous investments made in maternal and child health over the past few decades, 99 percent of children born today in the GCC countries will survive to age 5.

Learning-adjusted years of school (LAYS). Children in the GCC countries are expected to spend between 12.3 and 13.3 years in school but only learn the equivalent of 7.6 to 9.6 years. The results presented in table 1.1 indicate a learning gap between time spent in school and years of learning while in school. The gap across countries hovers around 4.0 years on average, with Kuwait having the highest gap, 4.8 years, and the United Arab Emirates having the lowest gap, 3.6 years. The quality of learning is the key factor in the relatively low HCI scores in the GCC countries.

TABLE 1.1 **Learning-adjusted years of school in the Gulf Cooperation Council countries, 2018**

COUNTRY	YEARS	LAYS	GAP
Bahrain	13.3	9.6	3.7
Kuwait	12.4	7.6	4.8
Oman	13.1	8.9	4.2
Qatar	12.3	8.5	3.8
Saudi Arabia	12.4	8.1	4.3
United Arab Emirates	13.1	9.5	3.6

Source: World Bank 2018.
Note: LAYS = learning-adjusted years of school.

TABLE 1.2 **Human Capital Index in the Gulf Cooperation Council countries, 2018**

COUNTRY	HUMAN CAPITAL INDEX	RANK
Bahrain	0.67	47
Kuwait	0.58	77
Oman	0.62	54
Qatar	0.61	60
Saudi Arabia	0.58	73
United Arab Emirates	0.66	49

Source: World Bank 2018.

Health. Some 91 percent of children age 15 in Oman and Saudi Arabia will survive to age 60, as will 92 percent in Kuwait, 93 percent in Bahrain and the United Arab Emirates, and 94 percent in Qatar. These outcomes are good but can be improved by reducing premature deaths from transport injuries and noncommunicable diseases. Children not stunted account for 95 percent of all children in Kuwait and 86 percent in Oman, but this metric is not measured in the other GCC countries.

The resulting scores for the GCC countries show wide variation. Bahrain has the highest HCI score, 0.67, ranking 47th in the world, followed by the United Arab Emirates (0.66, 49th), Oman (0.62, 54th), Qatar (0.61, 60th), Saudi Arabia (0.58, 73rd), and Kuwait (0.58, 77th) (table 1.2). These scores mean that a child born today in a GCC country will only attain between 58 percent and 67 percent of his or her full health, learning, and potential productivity. The rankings show a difference of 30 places between Bahrain and Kuwait.

HCI scores in the GCC countries are higher than their regional peers' scores but lower than the scores of their economic peers. Scores for human capital in the GCC countries rank at the top in the Middle East and North Africa (MENA) region and are higher than the MENA average of 0.56 (figure 1.1).[1] Over the past decade, the GCC countries have overtaken Jordan, Lebanon, and Tunisia in international standardized reading and mathematics tests. However, the GCC countries do not compare favorably with countries such as Germany, the Republic of Korea, and Singapore, which have similar income levels but far higher HCI scores. Instead, the scores in the GCC countries are similar to those in less wealthy nations, such as Mexico, Thailand, and Turkey.

Across the GCC countries, the HCI for girls is higher than that for boys. The gender gap across the different HCI components is not large except for the LAYS, which amounts to one full year on average.

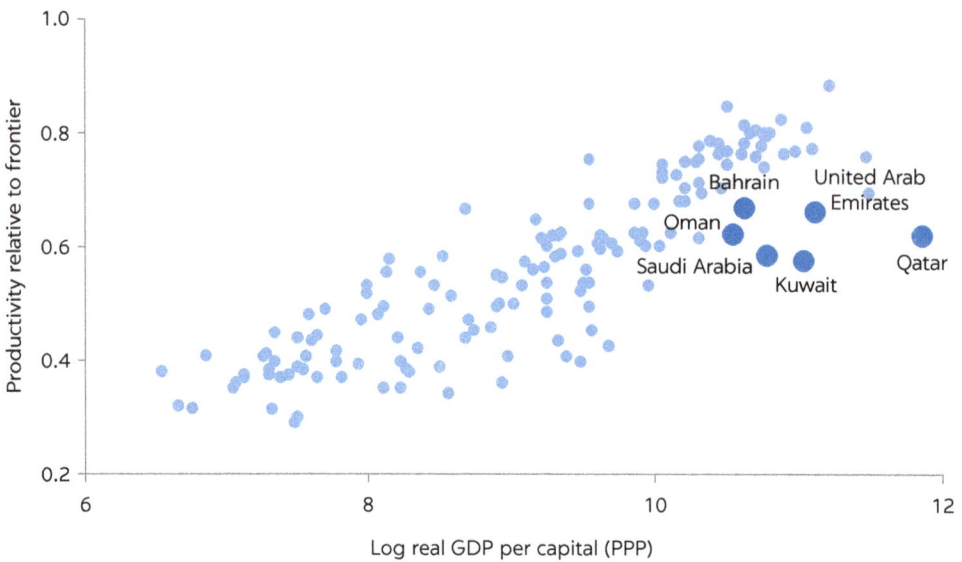

FIGURE 1.1

Human Capital Index: International benchmarking, 2018

Source: World Bank 2018.
Note: PPP = purchasing power parity.

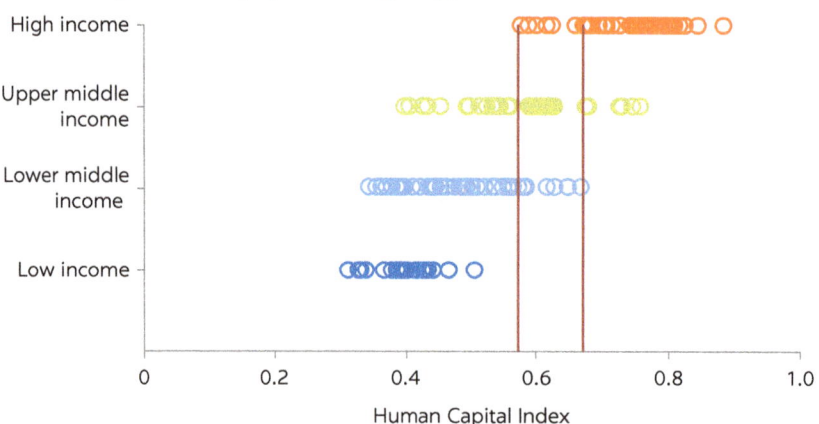

FIGURE 1.2

Human Capital Index, by income group, 2018

Source: World Bank 2018.

The HCI scores of the GCC countries are almost at the bottom of their high-income peers and at the level of middle-income countries (figure 1.2). Some upper-middle-income countries have higher scores than the GCC countries. These data suggest that more emphasis should be placed on ensuring value for money in public spending on education and health.

In October 2019, the World Bank launched an indicator to measure "learning poverty," which reflects the inability of a child to read and understand a simple text by age 10 (World Bank 2019a). The report emphasizes the importance of reading as a major contributing factor to improving human capital and as a foundational life skill because reading proficiency is an easily understood measure of learning, reading is a student's gateway to learning in every other area, and reading proficiency can serve as a proxy for foundational learning in other subjects, in the same way that the absence of child stunting is a marker of healthy early childhood development (World Bank 2019a).

As with the HCI, the GCC countries are doing better than their regional peers on the learning poverty indicator, but for their income levels, they perform lower than their peers (World Bank 2019a). The percentage of GCC 10-year-olds who cannot read with understanding ranges from 32 percent in Bahrain to 51 percent in Kuwait and, although it is greater than 65 percent in several non-GCC countries such as Tunisia and the Arab Republic of Egypt—and as high as 95 percent in the Republic of Yemen—against countries with a similar gross domestic product (GDP) per capita, the GCC countries are lower on this measure than expected. For example, 38 percent of Saudi Arabia's 10-year-olds cannot read and understand a simple text, compared with just 2 percent in the Netherlands and Sweden, 4 percent in Canada, and 6 percent in Germany (all with GDP per capita rates similar to that of Saudi Arabia).

The GCC countries share common constraints to effective teaching and learning for reading literacy. For example, boys in the GCC countries significantly underperform girls, with some of the highest differences in the world. Like other MENA countries, the GCC countries differ from high-performing education systems, with an overemphasis on rote memorization, insufficient time given to reading instruction, a dearth of engaging children's literature in Arabic and a lack of a home culture of reading, and very low early childhood education enrollment rates. Details of the profile for each of the GCC countries are given in appendix B, which includes the HCI components and the learning profile brief, as well as the most recent Programme for International Student Assessment results for Qatar, Saudi Arabia, and the United Arab Emirates.

ACCELERATING HUMAN CAPITAL FORMATION: A LIFELONG APPROACH

The HCI has some limitations. First, it projects the future productivity of those who are born today (the *flow*) and does not take into consideration current workers or young people ready to enter the labor market (the *stock*). Second, it stops at the end of secondary school at age 18 and does not consider postsecondary education or beyond. Third, it does not measure morbidity from noncommunicable diseases that affect the productivity of the workforce. To accelerate the pace of human capital formation, the GCC countries need to address both the flow and the stock of current and future workers, as well as consider factors in human capital beyond those measured by the HCI, in a "lifelong" approach.

A lifelong approach to human capital formation depends on recognizing the potential of the entire population. In figure 1.3, the center circle contains children age 0 to 18 years, reflecting the HCI components, where more investments could be made for child survival, learning, prevention of stunting, and adult survival. The next circle shows the age group 0 to 25 years, when countries need to invest in high-quality early child development, improve tertiary education outcomes, modernize vocational training, reduce transport injuries, and reduce risk factors for noncommunicable diseases among youth. The outer circle represents those older than age 25, when strategies are needed to encourage lifelong learning, develop skills, and address labor market distortions; it also reflects the importance of encouraging women to participate in the labor force, improving social safety nets, and using technologies for improving human capital outcomes.

FIGURE 1.3
A lifelong approach to human capital: Realizing the full potential of a productive population

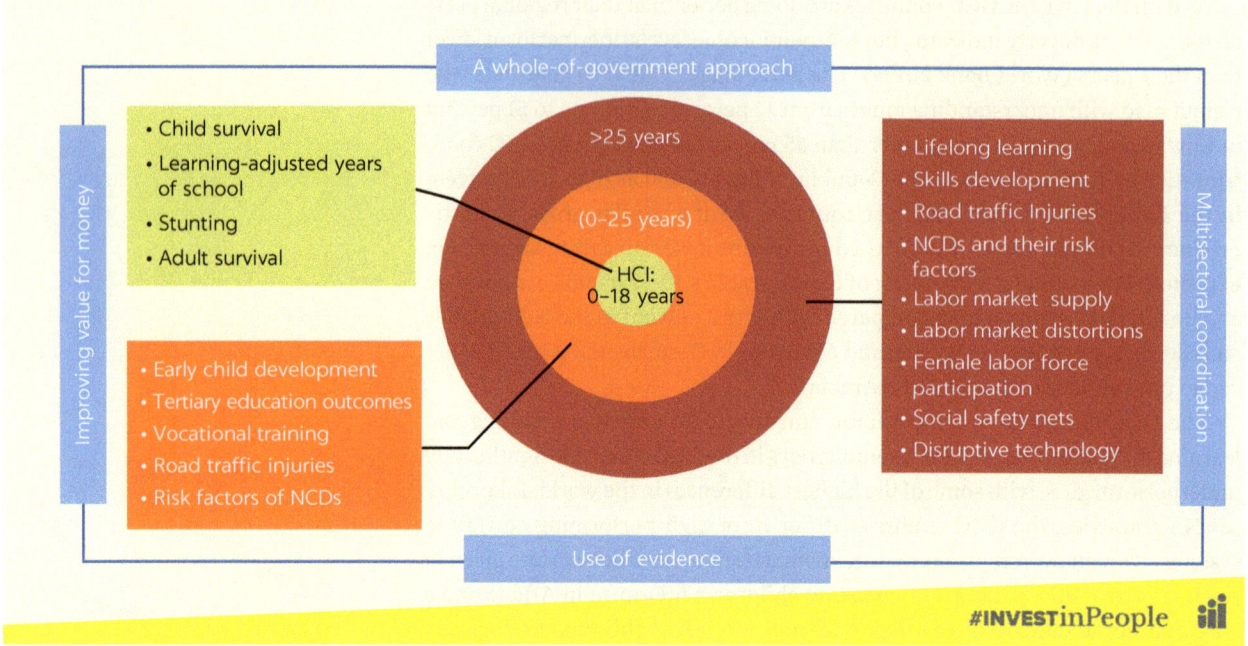

Source: Adapted from El-Saharty 2018.
Note: HCI = Human Capital Index; NCDs = noncommunicable diseases.

These strategies for a lifelong approach to human capital formation focus on improving value for money in human capital investment and on strengthening governance, which includes regulatory and institutional frameworks from sectors both within and outside government.

Effective implementation of these strategies requires the adoption of a "whole-of-government" approach for policy coordination across sectors, with a focus on improving value for money and the use of evidence. For example, investing in early child development will require collaboration between health, education, social protection, and family welfare government departments or ministries. Private sector partnerships are also critical because governments often do not have sufficient financial and technical resources with which to pursue these strategies. Furthermore, governments need community engagement strategies to gain support for reforms. Additionally, partnering with international organizations will allow governments to benefit from global best practices and develop informed, country-specific policies. Improving efficiency in public spending to increase returns on investment is particularly relevant for the GCC countries. Finally, improving data collection, analysis, and use is important to ensure that policy formulation is based on evidence and that midcourse adjustments are better guided.

HUMAN CAPITAL AND COVID-19

COVID-19, which began in China in late 2019 and became a pandemic by mid-March 2020, has reached 188 countries and territories, with more than 7 million infections and more than 403,000 deaths as of June 8, 2020.[2]

To prevent the spread of infection, many governments have implemented transmission control measures such as lockdowns and travel bans to "flatten the pandemic curve." In parallel, to mitigate the resulting adverse economic and social impacts, governments have taken monetary, fiscal, and structural measures to "flatten the recession curve."

The disease and GCC countries' responses, including those for the longer term, are detailed in chapter 4.

NOTES

1. While HCI scores are not currently disaggregated between GCC country nationals and nonnationals, PISA 2018 student assessments show immigrant students scoring significantly higher, on average, than their nonimmigrant peers in the GCC countries. On reading performance (tested in the language of instruction), immigrant students score an equivalent of 1 year of schooling above native students in Saudi Arabia, 2.5 years in Qatar, and 3 years in the United Arab Emirates.
2. "COVID-19 Dashboard by the Center for Systems Science and Engineering (CSSE) at Johns Hopkins University (JHU)," consulted April 24 (https://coronavirus.jhu.edu/map.html).

REFERENCES

Cunningham, Wendy, and Paula Villaseñor. 2016. "Employer Voices, Employer Demands, and Implications for Public Skills Development Policy Connecting the Labor and Education Sectors." *World Bank Research Observer* 31 (1): 102–34.

Deming, David J. 2017. "The Growing Importance of Social Skills in the Labor Market." *Quarterly Journal of Economics* 132 (4): 1593–640.

El-Saharty, Sameh. 2018. "Human Capital in the GCC Countries: Towards a Sustainable and Diversified Economy." Paper presented at the Kuwait Public Policy Center on November 28, 2018.

Gertler, Paul, James Heckman, Rodrigo Pinto, Arianna Zanolini, Christel Vermeersch, Susan Walker, Susan M. Chang, and Sally Grantham-McGregor. 2014. "Labor Market Returns to an Early Childhood Stimulation Intervention in Jamaica." *Science* 344 (6187): 998–1001.

Hanushek, Eric A., Guido Schwerdt, Simon Wiederhold, and Ludger Woessmann. 2017. "Coping with Change: International Differences in the Returns to Skills." *Economics Letters* 153 (April): 15–19.

Hanushek, Erik A., and Ludger Woessmann. 2015. *The Knowledge Capital of Nations: Education and the Economics of Growth*. CESifo Book Series. Cambridge, MA: MIT Press.

Krueger, Dirk, and Krishna B. Kumar. 2004. "Skill-Specific Rather Than General Education: A Reason for US-Europe Growth Differences?" *Journal of Economic Growth* 9 (2): 167–207.

Lange, Glenn-Marie, Quentin Wodon, and Kevin Carey, eds. 2018. *The Changing Wealth of Nations 2018: Building a Sustainable Future*. Washington, DC: World Bank.

World Bank. 2016. *World Development Report 2016: Digital Dividends*. Washington, DC: World Bank.

World Bank. 2018. "Human Capital Project." https://www.worldbank.org/en/publication/human-capital.

World Bank. 2019a. *Ending Learning Poverty: What Will It Take?* Washington, DC: World Bank.

World Bank. 2019b. *World Development Report 2019: The Changing Nature of Work*. Washington, DC: World Bank.

2 Four Main Challenges in Human Capital Formation

Four pressing challenges impede the accumulation of human capital in the Gulf Cooperation Council (GCC) countries: poor learning outcomes, the mismatch between education outcomes and labor market needs, relatively high adult mortality and morbidity, and a unique labor market. Some potential responses by GCC governments to these and many other considerations are outlined in their "Vision" statements (appendix A).

POOR LEARNING OUTCOMES

Despite substantial public investment in education, students across the GCC demonstrate lower levels of learning than students in other countries of similar income levels. The Trends in Mathematics and Science Study (TIMSS) and Progress in International Reading Literacy Study (PIRLS) are two common international assessments used to measure the learning of school-age children. In TIMSS, all six GCC member countries score lower than other high-income countries (figure 2.1).

On the grade 4 mathematics assessment, for example, the proportion of students achieving at least the lowest of the four international benchmarks ranges from 23 percent in Kuwait to 72 percent in Bahrain—well below the international median of 93 percent who reached the lowest benchmark.[1] By contrast, in high-performing countries such as Japan, the Republic of Korea, the Netherlands, and Singapore, the proportion of students reaching the "low" international benchmark exceeds 99 percent. The trends are similar in other assessed subjects (science and reading) as well as at grade 8—where GCC students perform closer to, but still below, the international average (figure 2.2).

In December 2019, the Organisation for Economic Co-operation and Development (OECD) published the latest results of its triennial assessment of 15-year-olds' skills in reading, mathematics, and science under the Programme for International Student Assessment. The results for three GCC countries—presented in box 2.1 and in more detail in appendix B—were largely in line with the results of other recent international assessments, such as TIMSS and PIRLS.

FIGURE 2.1
TIMSS grade 4 mathematics performance and GDP per capita, 2015

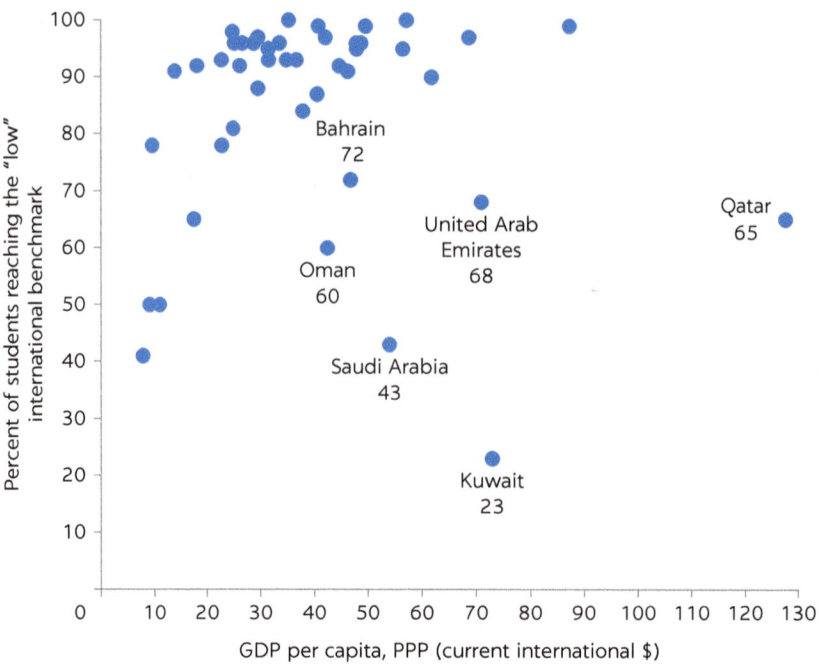

Source: World Bank EdStats database (https://datatopics.worldbank.org/education/), based on data from Trends in Mathematics and Science Study 2015.
Note: PPP = purchasing power parity.

FIGURE 2.2
Percentage of students in the Gulf Cooperation Council countries reaching the "low" international benchmark in TIMSS 2015 and PIRLS 2016, by subject

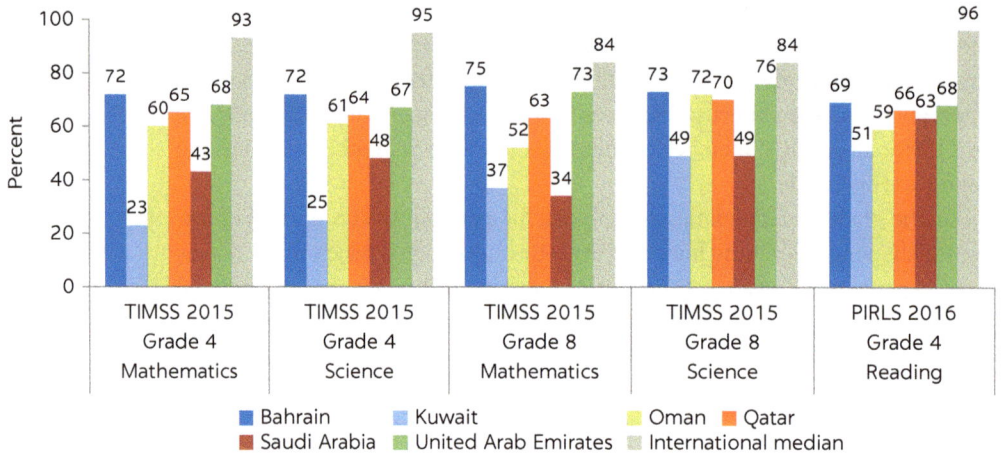

Source: World Bank EdStats database (https://datatopics.worldbank.org/education/), based on data from TIMSS 2015 and PIRLS 2016.
Note: PIRLS = Progress in International Reading Literacy Study; TIMSS = Trends in Mathematics and Science Study.

Although school enrollment rates are high, when adjusted for the quality of education that children receive, the effective educational attainment in the GCC countries is significantly lower. In recent decades, the GCC countries have made great strides in expanding access to schooling and ensuring gender parity. Yet schooling is not the same as learning (World Bank 2018a). After adjusting for

BOX 2.1

Recent Programme for International Student Assessment results

Three Gulf Cooperation Council (GCC) countries—Qatar, Saudi Arabia, and the United Arab Emirates—were among the 79 economies participating in the Programme for International Student Assessment round administered in 2018 (Saudi Arabia took part for the first time). The results were not encouraging.

Although Qatar continued to show steady improvement in student performance, all three GCC countries scored far below the Organisation for Economic Co-operation and Development (OECD) average and below other high-income countries. Roughly half of 15-year-olds in the participating GCC countries were unable to demonstrate basic proficiency in reading, mathematics, and science. The shares of students reaching basic proficiency levels in the three subjects were as follows: Qatar, 49, 46, and 52 percent; Saudi Arabia, 48, 27, and 38 percent; and the United Arab Emirates, 57, 54, and 57 percent—compared with the OECD average of 77, 76, and 78 percent.

The GCC countries saw large and increasing learning gaps across several dimensions. Girls tended to outperform boys in reading by an average of two years of schooling; private school students outperformed their public school counterparts by the equivalent of two and a half years of schooling in Qatar and the United Arab Emirates, and by about one year in Saudi Arabia; and students from the top of the socioeconomic distribution scored two to three years of schooling above their peers from the bottom of the distribution.

Source: OECD 2019.

FIGURE 2.3
Learning-adjusted years of school in Gulf Cooperation Council countries, by gender, 2018

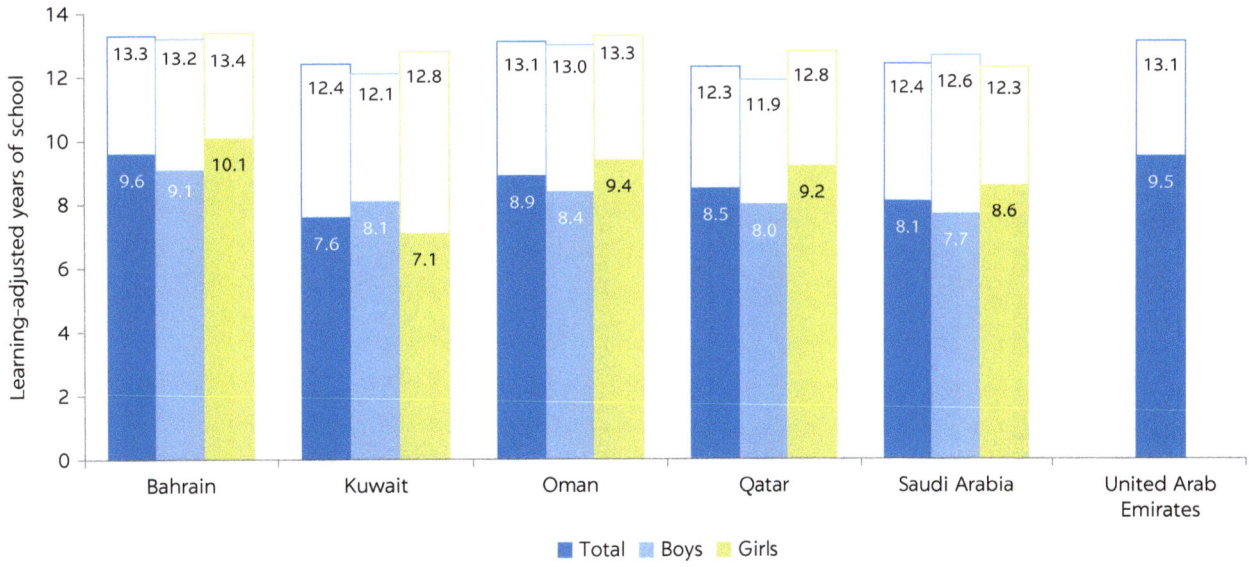

Source: World Bank 2018b.
Note: Gender-disaggregated enrollment data for the United Arab Emirates were not available when the 2018 Human Capital Index was prepared. Total bar height represents the expected years of school; solid color bar represents learning-adjusted years of school.

learning outcomes, the average educational attainment in the GCC countries declines from 13 expected years of school to 9 learning-adjusted years of school (LAYS) (figure 2.3). Moreover, gender parity in enrollment turns into gender disparities in effective schooling, with boys trailing girls in most GCC countries. An 18-year-old male is expected to complete about 12.6 years of schooling on average across the GCC countries; however, this corresponds to only 8.3 LAYS. The 12.9 years of expected schooling for females translate into just slightly more, 8.9 LAYS.

The GCC countries show substantial learning gaps between groups. Although nearly half of GCC students on average fail to gain the minimum understanding of mathematics, science, and reading (figure 2.4, panels a and b), the learning gaps between the top- and bottom-performing students are vast. Those in the 75th TIMSS percentile score on average 120 to 150 scale points higher than those in the 25th percentile in grade 4 math (panel a of figure 2.4). This gap is equivalent to approximately two TIMSS international benchmark levels (that is, the worst quarter of performers score below the "low" international benchmark, while the best quarter score near the "high" international benchmark). The top quarter of students in Bahrain are on par with average students in Canada, while the bottom quarter of Bahraini test takers are on par with those in Indonesia. The gender gap is also significant, with boys significantly underperforming girls. In grade 4 mathematics, male students in Saudi Arabia, Oman, Bahrain, and Kuwait scored often far below their female counterparts (panel b of figure 2.4). In grade 4 reading, the gender gaps are even wider in all the GCC countries—indeed, the difference between test scores for boys and girls in Saudi Arabia and Oman are the largest in the world.

Two further issues stand out: the gender learning gap and teacher absenteeism and tardiness. Two parallel school systems—one for boys and one for girls—lead to very different results in the classroom along gender lines, with girls seen as outperforming boys academically. Still, some countries have begun to experiment with the first few grades of schooling by moving to mixed-gender classes (boys and girls in the same classes) or to female teachers teaching boys as well as girls to see whether these practices can help close the gender learning gap.

FIGURE 2.4

TIMSS grade 4 mathematics performance gaps in the Gulf Cooperation Council countries, 2015

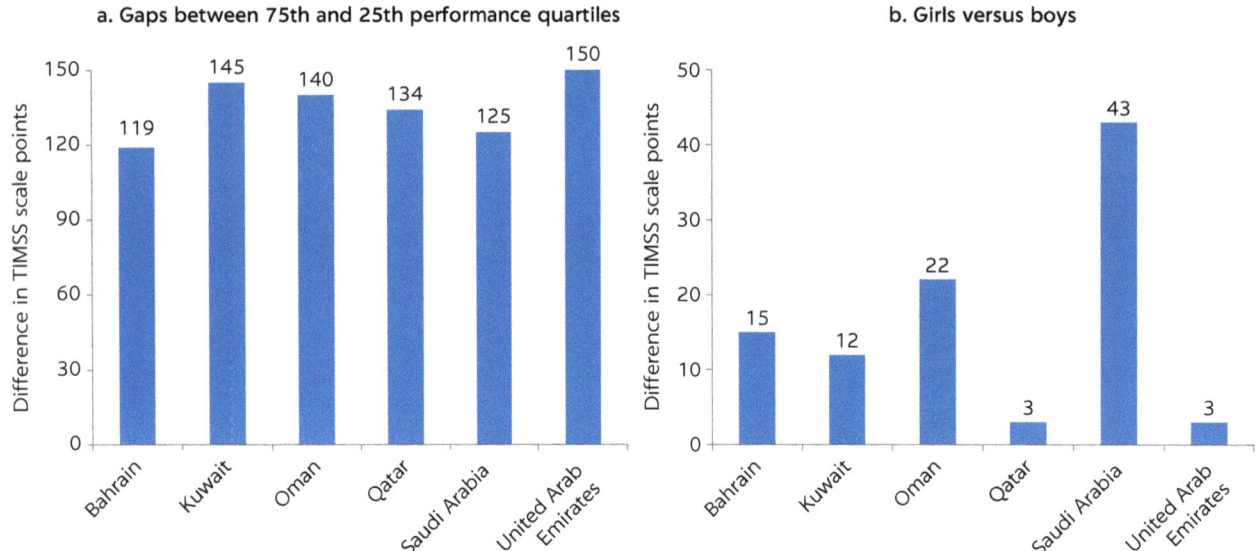

Source: World Bank EdStats database.
Note: All gaps are statistically significant except between girls and boys for grade 4 mathematics in Qatar and the United Arab Emirates. By comparison, (1) 75 points is equivalent to the difference between successive international benchmarks (for example, "low" and "intermediate") on the TIMSS scale; (2) the average gender gap in grade 4 mathematics among all countries participating in TIMSS 2015 was zero points; (3) the gender gaps in grade 4 reading in PIRLS 2016 for Gulf Cooperation Council member countries ranged from 30 points in the United Arab Emirates to 65 points in Saudi Arabia (versus an international average of 19 points). PIRLS = Progress in International Reading Literacy Study; TIMSS = Trends in Mathematics and Science Study.

TABLE 2.1 **Percentage of grade 4 students whose principals report that teacher absenteeism or tardiness is a serious or moderate problem, 2015**

COUNTRY	TEACHER ABSENTEEISM		TEACHERS ARRIVING LATE OR LEAVING EARLY	
	SERIOUS PROBLEM	MODERATE PROBLEM	SERIOUS PROBLEM	MODERATE PROBLEM
Bahrain	16	12	11	8
Kuwait	28	25	15	23
Oman	30	18	14	13
Qatar	10	10	9	4
Saudi Arabia	27	26	18	21
United Arab Emirates	9	12	4	5
TIMSS average	**7**	**8**	**5**	**5**

Source: IEA 2015.
Note: TIMSS = Trends in Mathematics and Science Study.

Teacher absenteeism and tardiness are common. According to reports by school principals quoted in TIMSS 2015, 53 percent of grade 4 students in Kuwait and Saudi Arabia attend schools where teacher absenteeism is a serious or moderate problem. The proportions are lower in other GCC countries but still exceed the TIMSS combined (that is, serious and moderate) international average of 15 percent (table 2.1). By comparison, only a combined 2 percent of students in the world's top-performing countries attend schools where teacher absenteeism is a problem. Similar trends are reported for teachers arriving late or leaving early: a combined 39 percent in Saudi Arabia, 38 percent in Kuwait, 27 percent in Oman, and 9 to 20 percent in the other GCC countries—compared with an international average of 10 percent.

Addressing these challenges requires the right mix of autonomy and accountability at the school level. Teachers and principals in the GCC report having relatively low levels of decision-making authority on basic school management and instructional decisions, such as formulating the school budget and selecting the appropriate instructional materials to be used in their school (OECD 2016). Without the autonomy to manage their schools and the right mix of accountability mechanisms to ensure that teachers show up to work and can teach effectively, school principals remain an underutilized resource in some GCC education systems.

MISMATCH BETWEEN EDUCATION OUTCOMES AND LABOR MARKET NEEDS

A 2018 World Bank report identified four "tensions" holding back education systems in many countries in the Middle East and North Africa region (World Bank 2018c). Among the complex interactions, behavioral norms, and ideological differences in the region, four sets of tensions are in play between credentials and skills, discipline and inquiry, control and autonomy, and tradition and modernity (figure 2.5). These tensions are embedded in the region's history, culture, and political economy. They define social and political relations and shape education policy; often, the impact they have on society, school, and the classroom prevents national education systems from evolving to deliver the skills that prepare students for their future.

FIGURE 2.5
Four tensions holding back education systems in the Gulf Cooperation Council countries

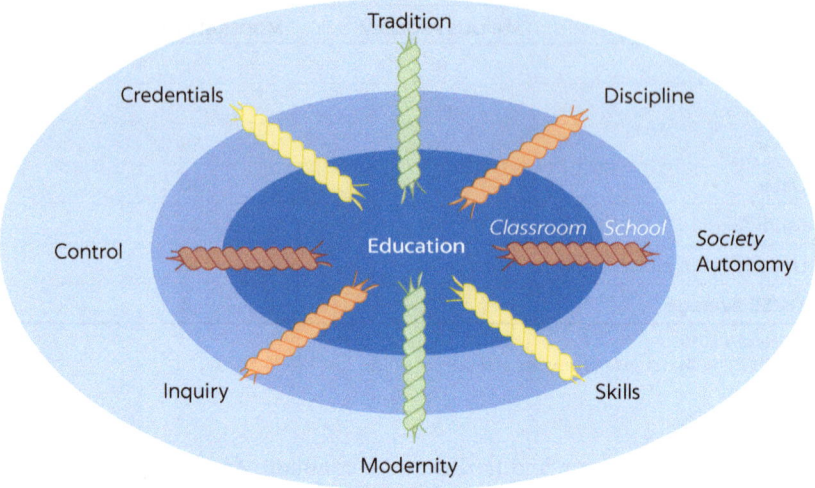

Source: World Bank 2018c.

FIGURE 2.6
Gulf Cooperation Council countries stuck in a credentialist equilibrium

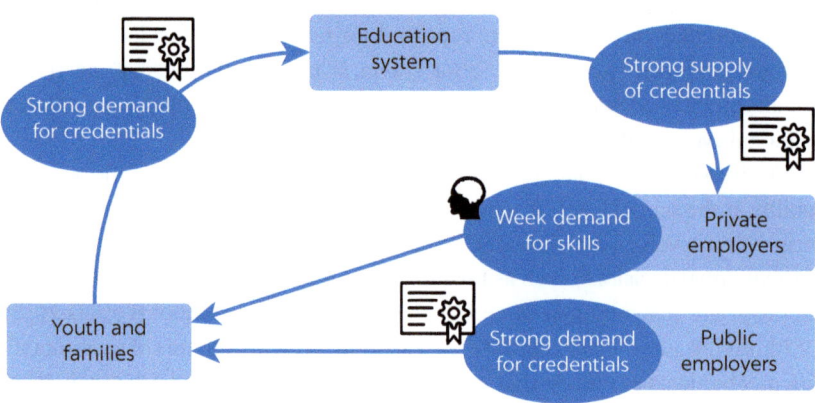

Source: World Bank 2018c.

The tension between credentials and skills leaves countries stuck in a "credentialist equilibrium." GCC governments have placed little pressure on educational institutions to ensure that graduates possess skills relevant to the labor market. Attaining credentials—a diploma, degree, or certificate—is emphasized more than acquiring skills, and is reinforced by the strong historical preference for public sector employment. In many GCC countries, such employment is guaranteed for anyone who obtains enough credentials, resulting in a credentialist equilibrium in which public sector employers communicate their strong demand for credentials, while the private sector communicates weak signals for the relevant skills needed (figure 2.6).

Students and families respond to these weak market signals by focusing more on the credentials and less on the skills that these credentials should represent (Salehi-Isfahani 2012). As a result, the outcomes produced by the education system—reflected in the graduates' credentials—can bear little resemblance to the demand for skills being communicated by private sector employers (Assaad, Krafft, and Salehi-Isfahani 2017).

The second tension, between discipline and inquiry, is evident in pedagogical and curricular norms predominant in GCC education systems. Public school instruction in the six countries tends to emphasize rote memorization over critical thinking and other twenty-first-century skills. Modern methods of teaching and learning, which emphasize critical thinking and inquiry, and the development of key twenty-first-century skills—such as problem solving, collaborative teamwork, and socioemotional and digital skills—remain largely out of favor. According to TIMSS 2015 data, roughly half of grade 8 science students in the GCC countries (ranging from 42 percent in Qatar to 57 percent in Saudi Arabia) reported being asked to memorize specific facts and principles in nearly every lesson. By comparison, the international average for this indicator was 30 percent, and in top-performing systems only 10 percent of students reported memorization as being a common instructional practice (figure 2.7).

The third tension, between control and autonomy, is usually associated with the debate on decentralization of services. The struggle in the balance of power between central ministries, regional offices, and schools is apparent in several GCC countries. Saudi Arabia, for example, has taken initial steps toward empowering local education directorates, but more substantive decentralization of decision-making control remains elusive. The goal of decentralization is typically to improve governance by fostering autonomy, accountability, and responsiveness to local conditions and needs. These attributes, in turn, can improve the quality of service delivery and student learning outcomes. However, a long history of centralized decision-making in the GCC countries makes it difficult to find the right balance between control and autonomy to ensure that education systems produce graduates with skills aligned to local needs.

Relatedly, the fourth tension, between tradition and modernity, holds back some key education system reforms. Although modernization of physical infrastructure and school equipment has taken place, the learning process itself remains very traditional in most GCC countries. Prevailing societal views on the primary purpose of education—to succeed in exams that allow students to obtain credentials—remain rooted in the traditions of the twentieth century and long before.

FIGURE 2.7

Percentage of grade 8 students asked to memorize science facts and principles for every lesson or almost every lesson, 2015

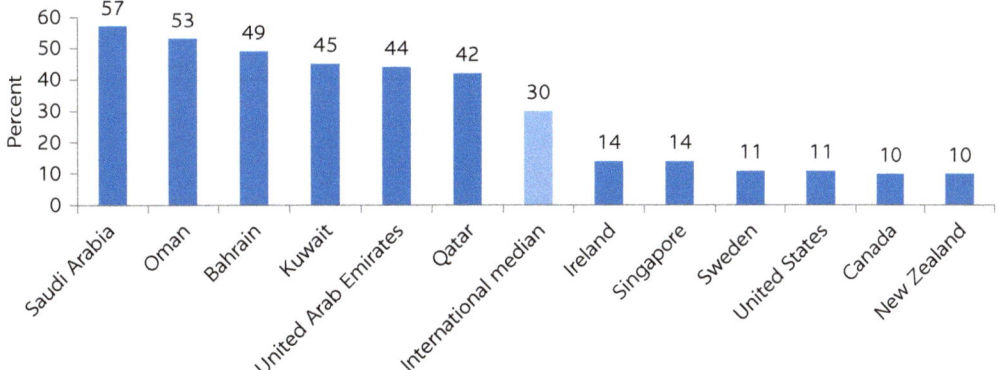

Source: Trends in Mathematics and Science Study 2015 data, reproduced in World Bank 2018c.

RELATIVELY HIGH ADULT MORTALITY AND MORBIDITY

In 2016, average life expectancy at birth in the GCC countries was about 76 years, an increase of about 23 years in slightly more than five decades. Growing incomes and increased access to education and health care have all contributed to longer life spans (table 2.2). Nevertheless, adults between the ages of 15 and 60 die at a rate of 2.2 for every 1,000 people, and on average almost 19,000 disability-adjusted life years (DALYs) are lost for every 100,000 people due to ill health, disability, or early death (IHME 2017). These years could have been spent contributing to the overall productivity, income, and growth of the GCC economies.

The main drivers of mortality and morbidity in the GCC countries are non-communicable diseases (NCDs) and transport injuries (TIs). In the past 50 years, as the GCC countries have controlled communicable diseases and maternal and perinatal health complications, NCDs have become the leading cause of death, accounting for 71.5 percent of the total (table 2.3). The top cause of NCD-related deaths in the GCC countries is cardiovascular disease, similar to elsewhere in the world. Other leading causes of death include cancer, diabetes, kidney disease, neurological disorders, and chronic respiratory disease (IHME 2017). NCDs are also leading causes of disability in the GCC countries: NCDs account for

TABLE 2.2 **Life expectancy, 2016, and adult mortality and disability-adjusted life years, 2017, in the GCC countries**

COUNTRY	LIFE EXPECTANCY AT BIRTH, TOTAL (YEARS)	ADULT (15–60) MORTALITY RATE (DEATHS PER 1,000 POPULATION)	ADULT (15–60) (DALYs LOST OUT OF 100,000 POPULATION)
Bahrain	76.90	2.16	18,276.92
Kuwait	74.69	1.78	16,794.71
Oman	77.03	2.47	19,820.74
Qatar	78.18	1.34	16,312.91
Saudi Arabia	74.56	2.75	20,104.67
United Arab Emirates	77.26	2.54	22,483.75
GCC countries	**76.43**	**2.17**	**18,965.62**

Sources: IHME 2017; World Bank databank 2016.
Note: GCC = Gulf Cooperation Council; DALYs = disability-adjusted life years; OECD = Organisation for Economic Co-operation and Development.

TABLE 2.3 **Percentage of total deaths and DALYs caused by NCDs and TIs**

	PERCENTAGE OF TOTAL DEATHS			PERCENTAGE OF TOTAL DALYs		
	NCDs		TIs	NCDs		TIs
COUNTRY	1990	2016	2016	1990	2016	2016
Bahrain	77.31	83.97	4.15	70.54	82.31	3.27
Kuwait	52.75	76.11	7.41	56.23	79.34	4.91
Oman	56.78	66.67	17.86	52.46	69.74	12.74
Qatar	66.04	65.66	16.38	67.11	76.28	8.22
Saudi Arabia	52.44	67.35	12.86	48.21	71.00	9.66
United Arab Emirates	61.84	69.16	14.48	64.49	76.00	8.83
GCC member states	**61.20**	**71.50**	**12.19**	**59.84**	**75.77**	**7.90**

Source: IHME 2017.
Note: DALYs = disability-adjusted life years; GCC = Gulf Cooperation Council; NCDs = noncommunicable diseases; OECD = Organisation for Economic Co-operation and Development; TIs = transport injuries.

76 percent of DALYs, a measure that combines morbidity and mortality to calculate the years lost. In addition, in the GCC countries, TIs cause 12.2 percent of deaths on average and 7.9 percent of DALYs, a rate that is among the highest in the world.

Rising trends of NCDs and TIs are reflective of changes in both modifiable and nonmodifiable risk factors. The leading modifiable risk factors of NCDs and their metabolic precursors (high blood pressure, high cholesterol, high glucose levels, and obesity) include tobacco use, unhealthy diet, and lack of physical activity. Diets high in sugar and salt and low in vegetables and fruit, as well as insufficient physical activity, are leading risk factors for cardiovascular diseases and diabetes; tobacco use, including *shisha* (hookah), is a leading risk factor in chronic respiratory disease, cancer, and neurological diseases, such as strokes (figure 2.8). These rates are alarmingly high among youth. In Bahrain, Kuwait, Oman, and the United Arab Emirates, between one-third and one-half of young students are either overweight or obese (Kaneda and El-Saharty 2017). Moreover, dangerous driving has resulted in some of the highest TI rates in the world, with road traffic deaths ranging from 8 people per 100,000 in Bahrain, which is similar to the average for its income group (8), to 29 deaths per 100,000 people in Saudi Arabia.

The high burden of NCDs and TIs is impairing human capital, with the potential to increase pressure on public finances and heighten economic stress. Human capital potential and economic output are affected by NCDs and TIs in many ways, most importantly by reducing (1) the *quantity* of labor through the premature death of working-age individuals or their early retirement, and (2) the *quality* of labor in the form of losses in productivity, fewer days worked, and absenteeism. Complications resulting from cardiovascular diseases, chronic cancers, diabetes, and TIs can all lead to reduced productivity and ultimately a decrease in national income. Although spending per capita and as a share of GDP are below OECD averages, health expenditures have already grown since 2000 (figure 2.9). In a context in which public sector resources are already scarce, the high burden of NCDs and TIs requires a shift in focus toward organizational reform and efforts to generate greater value for money within the health sector to minimize economic stress.

FIGURE 2.8

Burden of disease attributable to six leading risk factors in the Gulf Cooperation Council countries, 2017

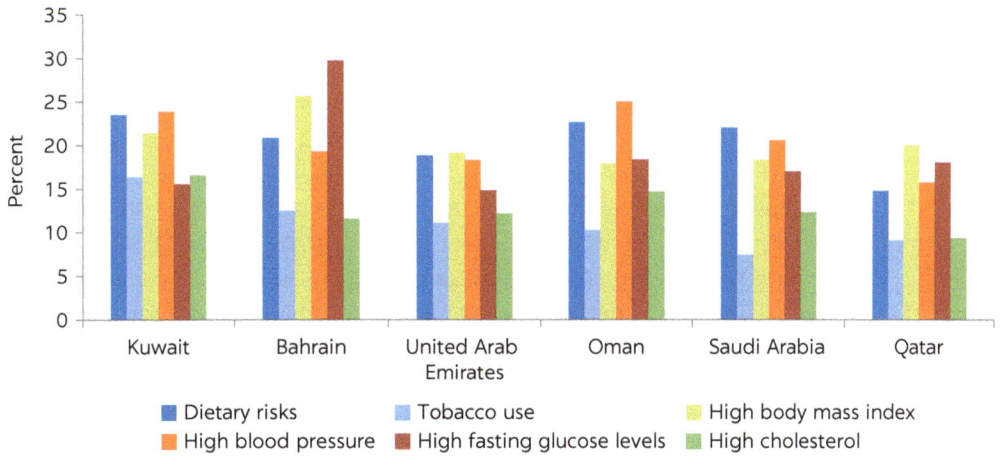

Source: IHME 2017.

FIGURE 2.9
Percentage of GDP spent on health in OECD and GCC member states

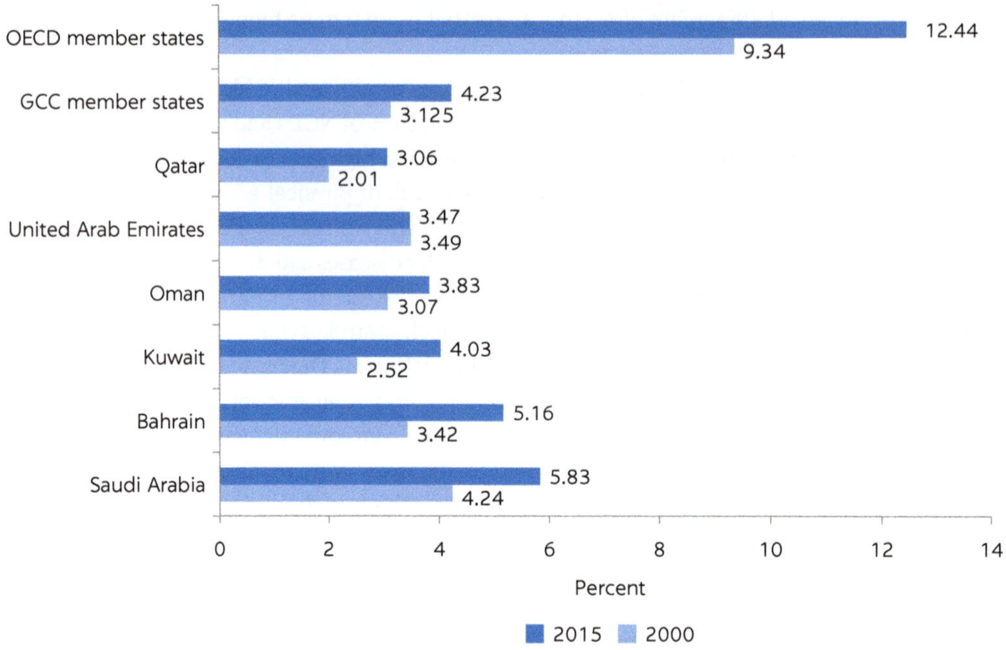

Region/Country	2015	2000
OECD member states	12.44	9.34
GCC member states	4.23	3.125
Qatar	3.06	2.01
United Arab Emirates	3.47	3.49
Oman	3.83	3.07
Kuwait	4.03	2.52
Bahrain	5.16	3.42
Saudi Arabia	5.83	4.24

Source: World Development Indicators, using data from https://datacatalog.worldbank.org/dataset/world-development-indicators.
Note: GCC = Gulf Cooperation Council; OECD = Organisation for Economic Co-operation and Development.

A UNIQUE LABOR MARKET

Unique features in labor markets in the GCC countries affect employment, especially in the private sector. Governments have legacy systems that allow the liberal entry of foreigners into private sector jobs, while virtually guaranteeing employment to nationals in government jobs. The liberal admission policies include regulating entry into the country, exit, residency, and work permits for noncitizens. In Qatar and the United Arab Emirates, foreigners make up about 90 percent of the total population, and in Saudi Arabia, more than 30 percent (figure 2.10). These foreigners perform 75 percent of all jobs in the private sector (IMF 2014), where most new jobs are likely to be created.

Public sector employment tends to be far more attractive than private employment. Its wages are more generous, making private sector employment unattractive for nationals. Public sector wages are between 180 percent and 250 percent of private sector wages in Saudi Arabia, Qatar, Bahrain, and Kuwait (panel a of figure 2.11). This wage disparity has led to nationals queueing for public sector jobs. A survey in 2016 found that 70 percent of GCC youth preferred a public sector job (ASDA'A Burson-Marsteller Arab Youth Survey 2016). In Saudi Arabia, for example, about 35 percent of total employment is in the public sector; in Kuwait, more than 25 percent; and in Qatar and the United Arab Emirates, about 20 percent (panel b of figure 2.11). In contrast, public sector employment as a share of total employment is about 18 percent in the OECD, 16 percent in the United Kingdom, 15 percent in the United States, 12 percent in Turkey, and 11 percent in Germany (OECD 2017).

FIGURE 2.10
Share of foreign nationals in the total population, Gulf Cooperation Council countries, circa 2016

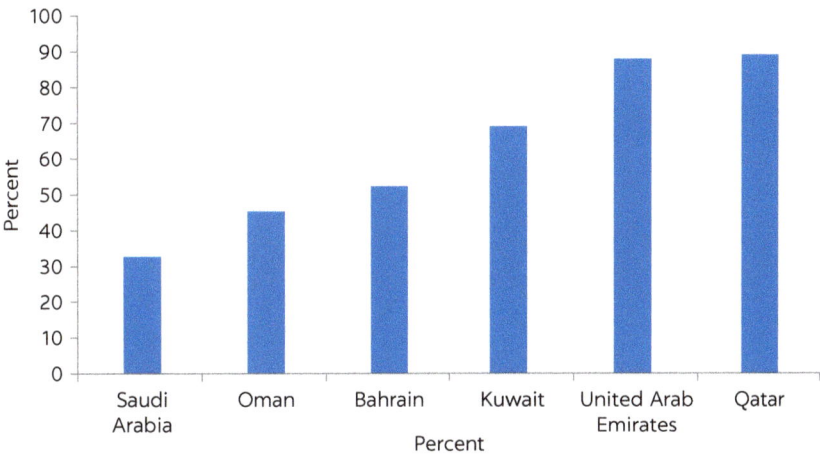

Source: Gulf Labour Markets and Migration Programme, using data from gulfmigration.eu (2016).

FIGURE 2.11
Public sector employment in the Gulf Cooperation Council countries

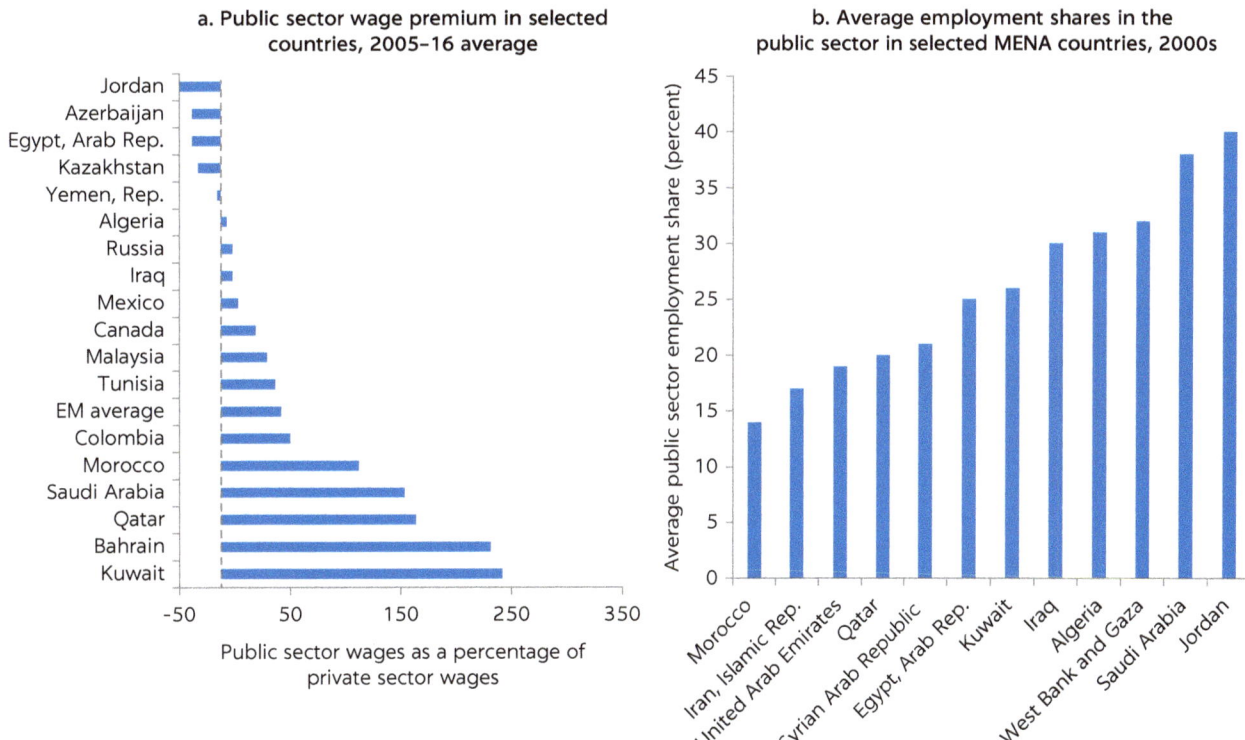

Sources: Tamirisa and Duenwald 2018 (panel a); World Bank 2013 (panel b).
Note: EM = emerging market; MENA = Middle East and North Africa.

Furthermore, female labor force participation is low (figure 2.12). Female labor force participation of 22 percent among those age 15 and older in Saudi Arabia and 30 percent in Oman is particularly low relative to 60 percent in the OECD countries. Only Qatar's female labor force participation rate of 58 percent is close to the OECD average. Moreover, women who work in a GCC country are

FIGURE 2.12
Female labor force participation versus income in the Gulf Cooperation Council countries

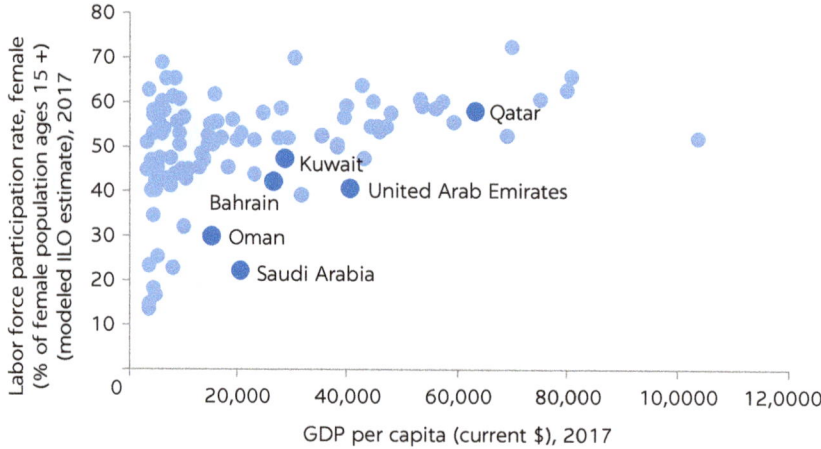

Source: World Development Indicators, using data from https://datacatalog.worldbank.org/dataset/world-development-indicators.

more likely to engage in low-productivity activities, to be unpaid family workers, to be restricted to relatively low-paid occupations and sectors, and to earn significantly less than similarly qualified men. Thus, the strong educational achievements seen among girls do not translate into strong employment outcomes, raising the issue of untapped human capital (World Bank 2019). Among the more than 60 countries that participated in the TIMSS, the six GCC countries had the largest gender disparities in student achievement, with girls significantly outperforming boys.

Several reasons have been identified for the low female labor force participation rate in the GCC countries.[2] The top four are (1) the "double burden" syndrome, which describes women who balance work and domestic responsibilities (29 percent); (2) lack of appropriate infrastructure—for example, restrictions associated with lack of transportation or women-only facilities (28 percent); (3) lack of family public policy or services, such as childcare options (26 percent); and (4) family or social expectations that prevent women from working (22 percent) (Ellis, Marcati, and Sperling 2015). Although the double burden syndrome and the lack of family public policies or services are present in many countries around the world, they are more pronounced in the GCC countries. Moreover, the deficiencies in the physical infrastructure for including women in a company or firm, and the family or social expectations placed on women, are particularly acute in the GCC countries relative to OECD countries. The World Bank's Women, Business and the Law Index measures the critical effects of laws and regulations on gender equality and on the economic decisions that women make. The index scores range from 0 to 100, with 100 representing the best overall score for rights given to women in comparison with men. Among the GCC countries, Bahrain, Saudi Arabia, and the United Arab Emirates improved the most in the Women, Business and the Law index (World Bank 2020). However, all GCC countries have considerable potential to reduce the number of discriminatory laws that threaten women's economic security, career growth, and work-life balance.

NOTES

1. The "low" international benchmark on TIMSS and PIRLS corresponds to students having acquired the basic minimum knowledge expected of that grade level. (At the second-lowest "intermediate" benchmark, test takers can demonstrate the ability to apply that knowledge in a variety of situations.)
2. Exhibit 3 in "Promoting Gender Diversity in the Gulf" (https://www.mckinsey.com/business-functions/organization/our-insights/promoting-gender-diversity-in-the-gulf).

REFERENCES

ASDA'A Burson-Marsteller Arab Youth Survey. 2016. *8th Annual ASDA'A BCW Arab Youth Survey: Inside the Hearts and Minds of Arab Youth.* Dubai: ASDA'A Burson-Marsteller.

Assaad, Ragui, Caroline Krafft, and Djavad Salehi-Isfahani. 2017. "Does the Type of Higher Education Affect Labor Market Outcomes? Evidence from Egypt and Jordan." *Higher Education* 75 (6): 1–51.

Ellis, Tari, Chiara Marcati, and Julia M. Sperling. 2015. "Promoting Gender Diversity in the Gulf." *McKinsey Quarterly,* February.

IEA (International Association for the Evaluation of Educational Achievement). 2015. Trends in International Mathematics and Science Study—TIMSS 2015 database. Chestnut Hill, MA: IEA. https://timssandpirls.bc.edu/timss2015/international-database/.

IHME (Institute for Health Metrics and Evaluation). 2017. *Findings from the Global Burden of Disease Study.* Seattle: Institute for Health Metrics and Evaluation.

IMF (International Monetary Fund). 2014. "Labor Market Reforms to Boost Employment and Productivity in the GCC—an Update." International Monetary Fund, Washington, DC.

Kaneda, Toshiko, and Sameh El-Saharty. 2017. *Curbing the Noncommunicable Disease Epidemic in the Middle East and North Africa: Prevention among Young People Is Key.* Washington, DC: Population Reference Bureau.

OECD (Organisation for Economic Co-operation and Development). 2016. *PISA 2015 Results: Policies and Practices for Successful Schools.* Vol. 2. Paris: OECD.

OECD (Organisation for Economic Co-operation and Development). 2017. *Government at a Glance—2017 Edition: Public Employment and Pay.* Paris: OECD.

OECD (Organisation for Economic Co-operation and Development). 2019. *PISA 2018 Results: What Students Know and Can Do.* Vol. 1. Paris: OECD.

Salehi-Isfahani, Djavad. 2012. "Education, Jobs, and Equity in the Middle East and North Africa." *Comparative Economic Studies* 54 (4): 843–61.

Tamirisa, Natalia T., and Christoph Duenwald. 2018. *Public Wage Bills in the Middle East and Central Asia.* Washington, DC: International Monetary Fund.

World Bank. 2013. *Jobs for Shared Prosperity: Time for Action in the Middle East and North Africa.* Washington, DC: World Bank.

World Bank. 2018a. *Expectations and Aspirations: A New Framework for Education in the Middle East and North Africa.* Washington, DC: World Bank.

World Bank. 2018b. "Human Capital Project." https://www.worldbank.org/en/publication/human-capital.

World Bank. 2018c. *World Development Report 2018: Learning to Realize Education's Promise.* Washington, DC: World Bank.

World Bank. 2019. *World Development Report 2019: The Changing Nature of Work.* Washington, DC: World Bank.

World Bank. 2020. *Women, Business and the Law 2020.* Washington, DC: World Bank.

3 Four Strategies for Accelerating Human Capital Formation

Given the four main areas of human capital challenge outlined in chapter 2, this chapter proposes four strategies (to be considered alongside appendix A). The chapter includes recommendations based on evidence and good practices to accelerate human capital formation by (1) investing in high-quality early childhood development, (2) preparing youth for the future, (3) enabling greater adult labor force participation, and (4) creating an enabling environment for human capital formation. The Gulf Cooperation Council (GCC) countries are well placed to adopt such strategies.

INVESTING IN HIGH-QUALITY EARLY CHILDHOOD DEVELOPMENT

The period from before birth to about age 6 is critical for children's development. During this time, the building blocks of the brain are formed, and the child's environment stimulates brain development (for example, see World Bank 2018a). As a result, high-quality interventions during the early years can have higher returns on investment than remedial interventions aimed at young adults who lack the necessary foundational skills. Prioritizing investment in early childhood development (ECD) requires public spending to be targeted toward improving health and nutrition interventions for women and young children, encouraging parental and community involvement in promoting child development, and expanding access to high-quality preschool programs for all children (figure 3.1).

Ensuring that all children have a strong start in life

Well-targeted health and nutrition interventions are critical for ensuring the cognitive development of all children in the first months and years of life. These interventions include programs that provide access to prenatal and neonatal health services to all mothers and young children, that reduce malnutrition and stunting among vulnerable populations, and that ensure universal immunizations. Childhood stunting and mortality—two key elements measured by the Human Capital Index—are largely preventable. Extending existing programs to

FIGURE 3.1

Yielding high returns with investment in the early years

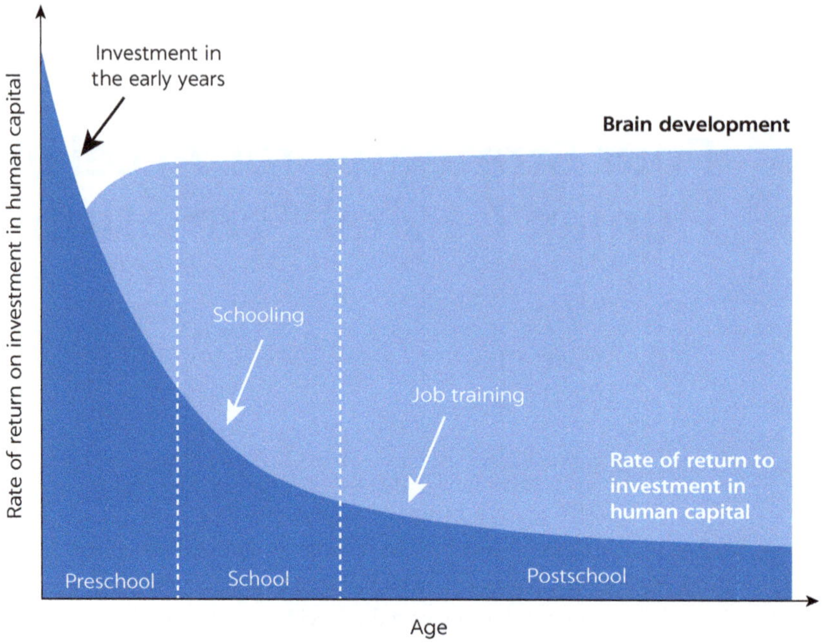

Sources: Carneiro, Cunha, and Heckman 2003; Martin 2012; World Bank 2018b.

cover the most marginalized populations is a straightforward way to prevent the loss of human capital in the early years of life (El-Kogali and Krafft 2015).

The role of parents and communities is equally important in ensuring that children develop physically and socioemotionally in the early years to maximize their human capital potential. Parental education programs that encourage parents to make the best evidence-based decisions for their child's development should aim to promote breastfeeding, a healthy diet, and effective ways to stimulate early cognitive and socioemotional development. Engaging communities in providing a healthy environment for young children can take many forms. Community and religious leaders, for example, could be trained in ECD strategies, which they can communicate to parents of young children. For instance, the Better Parenting project in Jordan trained *imams* and *khatibs* on how to teach parenting skills during or after Friday prayers, focusing specifically on reaching fathers of young children (El-Kogali and Krafft 2015).

Prioritizing public investment in the early years

The GCC countries have made large strides in expanding enrollment in preprimary education over the past four decades but need to make further progress. By 2016, 82 percent of children between the ages of 3 and 5 were enrolled in preschool in the United Arab Emirates (up from 32 percent in 1976). The gains have been equally impressive in Qatar (60 percent, up from 18 percent), Bahrain (55 percent, up from 9 percent), and Oman (57 percent, up from virtually zero). Saudi Arabia's preprimary enrollment rate has lagged, reaching only 25 percent in 2016, but the government is working to expand preschool access under Vision 2030. Most GCC countries should aim to reach the preschool enrollment levels of other high-income countries around the world (figure 3.2). The United Arab Emirates' private sector–driven model of early childhood education expansion might be a useful example (box 3.1).

Expanding ECD coverage alone is not sufficient, however; quality matters. High-quality ECD programs boost children's intellectual and social development, preparing them to enter primary school, ready to learn. Ample evidence shows that quality preschool education programs geared especially toward disadvantaged children have a positive impact on beneficiaries' earnings and even reduce crime (Elango and others 2015; Schweinhart and others 2005). These programs are also more cost-effective than other education interventions, such as reductions in class size, and help close performance gaps attributable to socioeconomic status, ethnicity, and geographic origin (Glewwe 2013; Heckman 2006). In contrast, low-quality ECD programs may be ineffective or even counterproductive (World Bank 2018a).

FIGURE 3.2

Preprimary education gross enrollment rates in Gulf Cooperation Council and high-income countries, 1976, 1996, and 2016

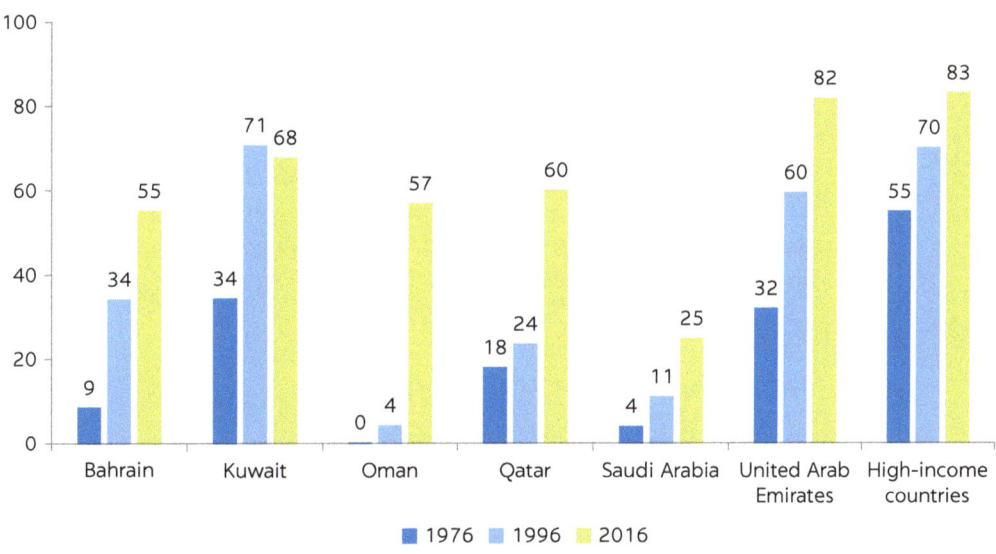

Source: World Bank EdStats database (based on data reported by countries to the UNESCO Institute for Statistics).
Note: The gross enrollment rate is calculated as the ratio of total enrollment, regardless of age, to the population of the age group that officially corresponds to the given level of education. Preprimary education typically corresponds to children ages 3 to 5 years.

BOX 3.1

Prioritizing early childhood education in the United Arab Emirates

As part of its Vision 2021, the government of the United Arab Emirates has set a target of 95 percent enrollment in preschool for the country's children by that year. This expansion aims to provide all children with a solid foundation for learning from an early age. As of 2017, more than 92 percent of children ages 4 and 5 were enrolled in public or private preschools, putting the United Arab Emirates at the head of the Gulf Cooperation Council class for preschool enrollment and showing a vast improvement from enrollment rates of about 30 percent in the 1970s and 60 percent in the 1990s.

Source: United Arab Emirates 2018.

Building foundational skills for school preparedness and future learning

The first three grades of school are key for ensuring that children build the skills necessary to participate in their education. Basic reading, writing, numeracy, and socioemotional skills lay the foundation for learning throughout a child's life and into adulthood. Children lacking these skills are at risk of falling behind, becoming disengaged from school, and not acquiring the more advanced skills increasingly demanded in today's changing labor market (World Bank 2018a). Early grade reading programs are effective at helping them acquire these skills (Graham and Kelly 2018).

To enhance children's readiness to learn, GCC governments could aim to align preprimary schooling with primary education to ensure a smooth transition for young children. Entering primary classrooms with a different educational philosophy (or language of instruction) can be a tough transition for young children. Moving from play-based, collaborative, child-centered learning to traditional teacher-centered instruction can undermine the positive impacts of even the most successful early childhood education programs. Therefore, aligning preschool and primary grade instructional styles is important, with both focusing on developmentally appropriate teaching and learning techniques. For example, the United Arab Emirates is in the process of aligning grades 1 and 2 of primary school with preprimary education, which consists of two years of kindergarten, to create a holistic early childhood education cycle covering all children from birth to age 8. Finland, New Zealand, and other Organisation for Economic Co-operation and Development countries have made similar efforts to align early childhood education with learning in the early grades (OECD 2012).

PREPARING YOUTH FOR THE FUTURE

This section moves beyond childhood to focus on building the human capital of youth before they enter the labor market. It considers the need to improve learning outcomes by focusing on the quality of education, by addressing specific needs of low-performing students, and by attracting better teachers. It also stresses linking education outcomes to labor market needs, and reducing health risk factors common among youth.

Improving learning outcomes

Better outcomes require greater efforts in three areas:

Focus on learning, not just schooling. To convert investment in education into economic growth, countries need to ensure that children attend school and learn the necessary skills that modern education systems should impart. Achieving this objective may require a shift in social norms and an agreement on a new social contract about the purpose of education, moving away from an outdated credentialist equilibrium toward a new "skills equilibrium" that focuses on competencies needed in the new economy.

Address the needs of low-performing students. Improved learning outcomes require concerted efforts focusing on low-performing students who are most at risk of failing to achieve key learning targets. In the GCC countries, these students are often male, rural, or from less advantaged families (such as those with less educated parents). Better learning outcomes also require teachers and school leaders to be empowered, and curricula and pedagogical practices to be modernized. Some schools and localities where low-performing students learn and live may need additional resources (financial, human, and physical). Additionally, far-reaching policy reforms may need to place the improvement of learning outcomes for societies' most marginalized children at the forefront of the education sector.

Attract the best into teaching, provide them with the right incentives, and empower teachers and school leaders. The teaching profession in some GCC countries is a job of last resort. Applicants to university education programs are often selected from the lower end of the admissions exam distribution. In systems in which boys are taught by male teachers, an equal number of male and female teaching applicants is needed. Yet—especially among male candidates—many of those entering the teaching profession do so only after being unable to secure other public sector jobs. Thus, the qualifications at entry and motivation on the job tend to be lower among male teachers, exacerbating lower quality instruction in boys' schools. Through a combination of rigorous selection into the education profession, appropriate incentives for good performance, and the necessary authority to teach and manage effectively, frontline actors in the GCC's education systems can play a key role in improving student learning outcomes.

Linking education outcomes to labor market needs

The education system should emphasize skills to meet the needs of the labor market. Continuing to teach the same subjects in the same way is unlikely to produce graduates who are well prepared for the jobs of the future. The nature of work is changing around the world and across the GCC, and education systems must adjust to meet these changes (World Bank 2019). This adjustment requires an alignment of key actors in society with common educational goals; a modernization of curricula, including for vocational education, technical education, and higher education; and a series of reforms beyond the education sphere to allow GCC societies to move toward a new skills equilibrium.

More specifically, governments will want to do the following:

Align curricula with in-demand skills. Across the world, curricular reforms are moving toward expressing education outcomes as skills to be developed over a lifetime and away from subject material or concepts to be memorized for an exam. Many top-performing education systems take a variety of approaches to developing and implementing skills- or competency-based curricula. In public schools in the United States, competency-based systems use state learning standards to determine academic expectations and define "proficiency" in a given course, subject area, or grade level. In several East Asian education systems (including those of Hong Kong SAR, China; Japan; the Republic of Korea; and Singapore), competency-based curricula aim to help students develop twenty-first-century skills by reducing the relative weight of subject-centered education.

Continue ensuring that legislative measures translate into practice in the classroom. The GCC countries have taken a legislative approach to education reform,[1] but could do more to adopt changes so that the needed skills are learned. Many classrooms in the GCC countries follow traditional teaching methods, including rote memorization, while the ability to think critically and ask questions is often discouraged. All teachers need to be capable of and willing to apply modern teaching methods to help students develop the necessary competencies for the changing nature of work in the twenty-first century (World Bank 2018a).

Encourage stakeholders to take a more active role. Policy makers should provide the leadership necessary for the education system to promote learning and skills, and should enable school leaders to create an educational environment conducive to learning and to empowering teachers. Teachers, in turn, should take responsibility for ensuring student learning, for monitoring and reporting results to parents and students, and for reducing their absenteeism rates. Parents can also do their part by ensuring that their children attend and complete school, as well as by supporting them at home to enable learning. Students must become curious and active learners who are responsible for their own educational success, and should demand accountability from teachers, school leaders, and policy makers. Finally, the job market, particularly private employers, should assume a more active role by sending clear signals to the education system and to parents regarding the skills that they demand of their current and future workers (World Bank 2018a).

Reducing health risk factors

The GCC region is going through a unique demographic period in which more than half of the population is under age 30. This demographic position presents a great opportunity for economic growth; however, an estimated two-thirds of premature deaths in adulthood result from childhood conditions and risky behaviors acquired during adolescence. Interventions that focus on the youth in the region can thus reduce noncommunicable diseases (NCDs) in later years and maximize the productive and economic benefits for the region.

Some GCC countries have taken steps, such as taxing tobacco products and sugary drinks (Saudi Arabia and the United Arab Emirates); banning tobacco advertising, promotion, and sponsorship (Qatar and Bahrain); and reducing the amount of salt in bread (Oman) (Kaneda and El-Saharty 2017). However, more measures are needed, including school health programs that emphasize nutrition, physical activity, and education on NCD risk factors and on avoidable traffic accidents. For example, measures should be strengthened to prohibit the sale of junk food and sugary drinks in school environments and to prevent the advertising of unhealthy products to children and adolescents. Ultimately, policies need to be adopted or scaled up that target both young people and those who influence them—online or offline—to ensure that supportive, reinforcing interventions and programs are in place. A focus on specific subpopulations susceptible to health risk factors—in particular, "catalytic populations" such as adolescents and youth—will be critical for maximizing economic potential.

ENABLING GREATER ADULT LABOR FORCE PARTICIPATION

Moving along the life cycle curve, this section suggests strategies for improving human capital formation among the adult population. The strategies relate to lifelong learning, female labor force participation, correcting the skills mismatch, and addressing the relatively high rate of adult mortality and morbidity.

Emphasizing lifelong learning

The changing nature of work in the modern economies of the GCC requires strong foundations for human capital and lifelong learning (World Bank 2019). How well countries cope with the demand for changing job skills depends on how quickly the supply of skills shifts. Countries can no longer wait for the next generation of school or university graduates (the flow of workers) to enter the labor market to meet the demands of a rapidly changing knowledge economy. They must ensure that access to lifelong learning opportunities is available to current workers (the stock of workers) for the entire duration of their productive lives. These opportunities can be offered through formal education systems (including short courses and certificate programs) as well as through on-the-job training opportunities and other upskilling programs geared toward adults.

Increasing female labor force participation

In the GCC countries, although girls outperform boys in school, female labor force participation rates are lower than male rates. Country-specific actions should be put in place to increase female participation, alongside some common strategies for all GCC countries.

Revise laws and regulations to encourage female labor force participation. First, steps could be taken to level the legal playing field so that the rules for employees and employers work equally for men and women. Second, work policies should be put in place to make it easier and less expensive to hire workers using flexible contracts. Although labor laws are flexible in the GCC countries, it is usually expensive or impractical for employers to hire workers on a part-time basis or on a temporary work contract. Such contracts are preferred by some women, and even some youth, as well as by employers who cannot make a business case for hiring workers long term or for paying all the benefits that go along with permanent or full-time work. Third, improvements should be made to parental leave policies to help ensure that women are better able to balance the double burden of home and work responsibilities.

Expand access to affordable and good-quality childcare. Affordable, good-quality childcare can enable women with children to work outside the home. Of course, enabling mothers to work is in addition to the many benefits preprimary enrollment have on children's success in school and later in adult life. Preprimary enrollment is very low in the GCC countries, although this situation can change; the United Arab Emirates has made impressive progress in recent years in this area. Still, the GCC countries have the potential to increase access to good-quality preprimary education.

Increase women's ability to become employed and succeed at work through active labor market programs. Not only are many women in the GCC countries out of the labor force, many have been unemployed for a long time, leaving them with outdated skills. To address this skills gap, especially given the changing nature of work, GCC governments could pilot active labor market programs, and scale them up when positive evidence of their impact is proven. Options might include short- and long-term training programs, depending on the needs of the client; on-the-job training through wage subsidy programs; and programs to foster and facilitate entrepreneurship, which is an area that is greatly underemphasized in the GCC countries. Although many GCC countries have active labor market programs, coverage is small relative to need, and, more generally, little is known about the programs' impacts.

Conduct media campaigns to address social norms and combat misconceptions and misperceptions about female employment. Documenting attitudes and providing positive role models can be helpful. For example, an interesting study in Saudi Arabia provides evidence that most young married men privately support female labor force participation outside the home, but these men also substantially underestimate support for female labor force participation by other men in this grouping (Bursztyn, Gonzalez, and Yanagizawa-Drott 2018). In addition, women who work tend to suffer from the double burden syndrome. Launching public awareness campaigns to reflect support and positive role models for women in the workforce can inspire women not already in the labor market to join it.

Ensure safety and provide women with women-only facilities, both in the workplace and during the journey to work. Countries have implemented policies that protect women in the workplace and have raised awareness about the legal consequences of harassment. To address safety during the journey to work, some countries around the world (the Arab Republic of Egypt, Japan, and Mexico, for example) provide women-only public transportation (World Bank 2013). Finally, providing women-only facilities can ensure that women are included and feel comfortable in the workplace. The GCC countries should consider emulating these approaches, subject to cultural norms.

Reducing the skills mismatch for unemployed or underemployed adults

Retraining can help address the mismatch between the skills attained in school and employers' needs. For the current workforce, upskilling and reskilling workers will require four actions: (1) a system to assess training needs, such as a profiling system that can provide clients with the appropriate intervention depending on their skills and demand for their skills; (2) technical and vocational education and training programs for people who require more intensive training, for example, reskilling; (3) short-term training programs to upskill workers (but with measurement of their effectiveness); and (4) on-the-job training programs, such as wage subsidy programs, which will help people receive training and much-valued work experience.

Reducing adult mortality and morbidity

Expanding or scaling up high-impact and cost-effective health interventions, and reshaping the way services are organized and delivered, will reduce adult mortality and morbidity. It is important to minimize NCDs and transport injuries and maximize human capital potential to reap both health and economic benefits in the GCC countries. The primary goals of such efforts should be to minimize diseases and injuries and prolong and enhance the life and productivity of working-age people, while slowing the acceleration of health care expenditures (as a share of GDP). A relative reduction in health care expenditures can be achieved by generating greater allocative efficiencies, focusing on cost-effective and targeted "best buy" interventions, and strengthening implementation efforts. Such efficiencies require a move away from costly traditional, curative models of care and toward those focusing on health promotion, prevention, early diagnosis, and evidence generation for planning and monitoring. Such models emphasize efficiency, quality, and equity; integrated health care network approaches; and population health care management approaches that deliver customized services at the individual, household, and population levels.

A wide array of interventions should be considered, even if many of them lie outside the health sector and therefore require multisectoral collaboration. Cost-effective interventions to address some of the behavioral risk factors of NCDs and transport injuries include bans, taxation, and regulation of the sale, promotion, or use of tobacco products and sugary drinks or of foods high in calories, saturated fat, or salt content. They include investments in infrastructure to make roads safer, enforce existing laws, and expand access and opportunities for recreational or physical activity. Within the health sector, strengthening primary care service delivery could help maximize the detection, monitoring, and management of biological risk factors, such as hypertension or diabetes. All the GCC countries have made some progress on such interventions but should now focus on further scaling them up. Most of these interventions require collaboration across sectors to ensure long-lasting healthy behaviors.

CREATING AN ENABLING ENVIRONMENT FOR HUMAN CAPITAL FORMATION

This section considers how the GCC countries can create an environment that would enable and encourage a productive population. It presents strategies related to effectively investing resources, taking a multisectoral approach in developing human capital, aligning social and political interests, and changing norms and behaviors.

Increasing value for money

Public spending on social sectors in the GCC countries would yield higher returns and better outcomes if its effectiveness and efficiency were improved. In the health sector, for example, reallocating resources from treatment to prevention could improve health outcomes. An excessively large portion of health spending covers higher-cost secondary and tertiary care services rather than targeting lower-cost prevention, promotion, and primary care services. More resources could be reallocated from expensive hospital care and treatment abroad toward well-targeted primary and secondary preventions that focus on creating and managing long-lasting healthy behaviors by individuals.

Whereas primary prevention programs in the health, education, social, or transport sectors should aim to prevent adverse health events from occurring in the first place, secondary prevention programs should aim to reduce the incidence, recurrence, or further health deterioration after an event has occurred. For example, in a model in which such programs are delivered by primary care practitioners, at-risk patients can be more efficiently screened for NCD-related risk factors, and patients with chronic diseases can be more effectively managed and monitored. In the education sector, shifting more resources toward early learning interventions and targeting public spending toward the neediest populations and low-performing students can generate greater returns in terms of improved learning outcomes than current spending patterns, which tend to overinvest in higher education.

Adopting a multisectoral approach to human capital

Improvements in human capital do not depend exclusively on social sector policies. Many of the strategies designed to improve human capital formation will require collaboration between different government entities (a "whole-of-government" approach) and the private sector, communities, and families. For example, investing in ECD will require collaboration between government departments or ministries responsible for health, education, social protection, and family welfare. Similarly, bridging the skills mismatch will require strong collaboration between the education and labor ministries and the private sector. Moreover, reducing health risk factors through, for example, tobacco taxation requires collaboration between the health and finance ministries.

Aligning social and political interests

Effective investment in human capital requires an alignment of political will and multiple interests in society (World Bank 2018a). Ideological polarization and entrenched special interests often hold countries back from enacting reforms that certain groups believe would reduce their power or ability to extract benefits (Khemani 2017; Kingdon and others 2014). One example from the education sector might be teachers benefiting from payments for private tutoring. In addition, teachers' unions may thwart reforms that would require teachers to work additional hours—or even show up and leave on time—or change their practices. Reforms can succeed if there is strong political will to implement them. An important step toward aligning political will with stakeholder interests would be an emphasis on shared values as part of the process of enacting reforms. In this way, stakeholders can be informed about the benefits of the reforms and feel as if their concerns have been heard, which could help reduce opposition to policy changes.

Changing norms and behaviors

Inefficient and outdated social norms can inhibit the reforms needed to accelerate human capital development (World Bank 2018a). Changing social norms is not easy, but it can be done. Raising awareness about the costs or inefficiencies of certain norms, or the benefits that would accrue to society from reforms, can help influence a shift in the social mind-set. However, such an effort would have to be based on credible evidence not connected to any ideological or political rhetoric, and would have to focus on real, substantial reforms and not minor changes in policies (Khemani 2017). Changing laws can also lead to a shift in norms (FIA Foundation for the Automobile and Society 2009); for example, laws on wearing seat belts in cars led to a shift in the social norm for driving safety and reducing fatalities from car crashes. However, enacting laws is not sufficient; laws must be enforced and positive behaviors encouraged. Meanwhile, a behavioral response to incentives in the short run can lead to longer-term shifts in behaviors and social norms. Two successful examples from the United States include sending text messages to "nudge" parents to register their children for ECD programs (Escueta and others 2017) and encouraging peer tutoring in higher education (Pugatch and Wilson 2018). The issues related to investing in early years, poorer learning outcomes of boys, low female labor force participation, or high prevalence of NCDs all have elements related to norms and behaviors. The examples discussed above show that norms and behaviors can be nudged to change with the right interventions, which can certainly be adapted to the GCC context.

NOTE

1. For example, Saudi Arabia's education legislation states that students should have the skills and knowledge to contribute to society economically and culturally and to build up their communities. The United Arab Emirates' curriculum states that its education system trains students for physical, intellectual, and emotional development, and prepares them for their future (UNESCO 2011). Through its Integrated Education Reform Program, Kuwait is transforming its curricula and instructional and assessment methods by focusing on the student, emphasizing applied knowledge, and adapting to different learning abilities.

REFERENCES

Bursztyn, Leonardo, Alessandra L. González, and David Yanagizawa-Drott. 2018. "Misperceived Social Norms: Female Labor Force Participation in Saudi Arabia." Working Paper 24736, National Bureau of Economic Research, Cambridge, MA.

Carneiro, Pedro, Flavio Cunha, and James J. Heckman. 2003. "Interpreting the Evidence of Family Influence on Child Development." Paper presented at Federal Reserve Bank of Minneapolis and McKnight Foundation conference, "Economics of Early Childhood Development: Lessons for Economic Policy," Minneapolis, October 17.

Elango, Sneha, Jorge Luis García, James J. Heckman, and Andrés Hojman. 2015. "Early Childhood Education." Working Paper 21766, National Bureau of Economic Research, Cambridge, MA.

El-Kogali, Safaa, and Caroline Krafft. 2015. *Expanding Opportunities for the Next Generation: Early Childhood Development in the Middle East and North Africa.* Washington, DC: World Bank.

Escueta, Maya, Vincent Quan, Andre Joshua Nickow, and Philip Oreopoulos. 2017. "Education Technology: An Evidence-Based Review." Working Paper 23744, National Bureau of Economic Research, Cambridge, MA.

FIA Foundation for the Automobile and Society. 2009. *Seat-Belts and Child Restraints: A Road Safety Manual for Decision-Makers and Practitioners.* London: FIA Foundation.

Glewwe, Paul, ed. 2013. *Education Policy in Developing Countries.* Chicago: University of Chicago Press.

Graham, Jimmy, and Sean Kelly. 2018. "How Effective Are Early Grade Reading Interventions? A Review of the Evidence." Policy Research Working Paper 8292, World Bank, Washington, DC.

Heckman, James J. 2006. "Skill Formation and the Economics of Investing in Disadvantaged Children." *Science* 312 (5782): 1900–02.

Kaneda, Toshiko, and Sameh El-Saharty. 2017. *Curbing the Noncommunicable Disease Epidemic in the Middle East and North Africa: Prevention among Young People Is Key.* Washington, DC: Population Reference Bureau.

Khemani, Stuti. 2017. "Political Economy of Reform." Policy Research Working Paper 8224, World Bank, Washington, DC.

Kingdon, Geeta Gandhi, Angela Little, Monazza Aslam, Shenila Rawal, Terry Moe, Harry Patrinos, Tara Beteille, Rumini Banerji, Brent Parton, and Shailendra K. Sharma. 2014. *A Rigorous Review of the Political Economy of Education Systems in Developing Countries.* London: UK Department for International Development.

Martin, Paul. 2012. "Responsabilidad Social Corporativa y Primera Infancia." Paper presented at Ministry of Development and Social Inclusion Semana de la Inclusión, Lima, October 21–24.

OECD (Organisation for Economic Co-operation and Development). 2012. *Starting Strong III: A Quality Toolbox for Early Childhood Education and Care.* Paris: OECD.

Pugatch, Todd, and Nicholas Wilson. 2018. "Nudging Study Habits: A Field Experiment on Peer Tutoring in Higher Education." *Economics of Education Review* 62: 151–61.

Schweinhart, Lawrence J., Jeanne Montie, Zongping Xiang, W. Steven Barnett, Clive R. Belfield, and Milagros Nores. 2005. *Lifetime Effects: The High/Scope Perry Preschool Study Through Age 40.* Ypsilanti, MI: High/Scope Press.

UNESCO (United Nations Educational, Scientific, and Cultural Organization). 2011. *World Data on Education: Seventh Edition 2010–11.* Paris: UNESCO International Bureau of Education.

United Arab Emirates. 2018. "Enrollment Rate in Preschools (Public and Private)." National Agenda 2021. https://www.vision2021.ae/en/national-agenda-2021/list/card/enrollment-rate-in-preschools-(public-and-private).

World Bank. 2013. *Jobs for Shared Prosperity: Time for Action in the Middle East and North Africa.* Washington, DC: World Bank.

World Bank. 2018a. *Expectations and Aspirations: A New Framework for Education in the Middle East and North Africa.* Washington, DC: World Bank.

World Bank. 2018b. *World Development Report 2018: Learning to Realize Education's Promise.* Washington, DC: World Bank.

World Bank. 2019. *World Development Report 2019: The Changing Nature of Work.* Washington, DC: World Bank.

4 The GCC Countries' Responses to COVID-19

In late 2019, a novel coronavirus (SARS-CoV-2), which causes the disease COVID-19, started to spread from Wuhan, the capital of China's Hubei province. The World Health Organization (WHO) declared the coronavirus outbreak a Public Health Emergency of International Concern on January 30, 2020, and a pandemic on March 11. As of June 8, COVID-19 had touched more than 188 countries and territories with more than 7 million infections and more than 403,000 deaths.[1]

To prevent the spread of infection, many governments have implemented transmission control measures, starting with "detect, test, isolate, and contact trace," which was then followed by more severe measures, such as lockdowns and travel bans to "flatten the pandemic curve." In parallel, governments have taken unprecedented monetary, fiscal, and structural measures to mitigate the resulting adverse economic and social impacts in an attempt to "flatten the recession curve." These measures have had mixed results, depending on how early and how forcefully countries have adopted them.

This chapter reviews the status of COVID-19 in the Gulf Cooperation Council (GCC) countries, the impact of the disease on human capital, measures taken by these countries, possible additional measures to consider, and public health considerations required to reopen economies.

BACKGROUND

The first case of COVID-19 in the GCC countries was detected in the United Arab Emirates on January 27, 2020, and most other GCC countries started to detect cases in late February. Since then, the GCC-wide number of cases has grown but the evolution has varied across the six countries. The pandemic curve has been rising slowly in Bahrain and Oman, but much faster in Kuwait, Qatar, Saudi Arabia, and the United Arab Emirates; that is, the pandemic curve is not flattening (figure 4.1).

As of June 8, 2020, the number of cases reached 101,914 in Saudi Arabia, followed by 68,790 in Qatar. The rate of tests per 1,000 population was highest in the United Arab Emirates and Bahrain. The GCC-wide case fatality rate was less

FIGURE 4.1
Trend of COVID-19 cases in the Gulf Cooperation Council countries, total of confirmed cases (as of June 8, 2020)

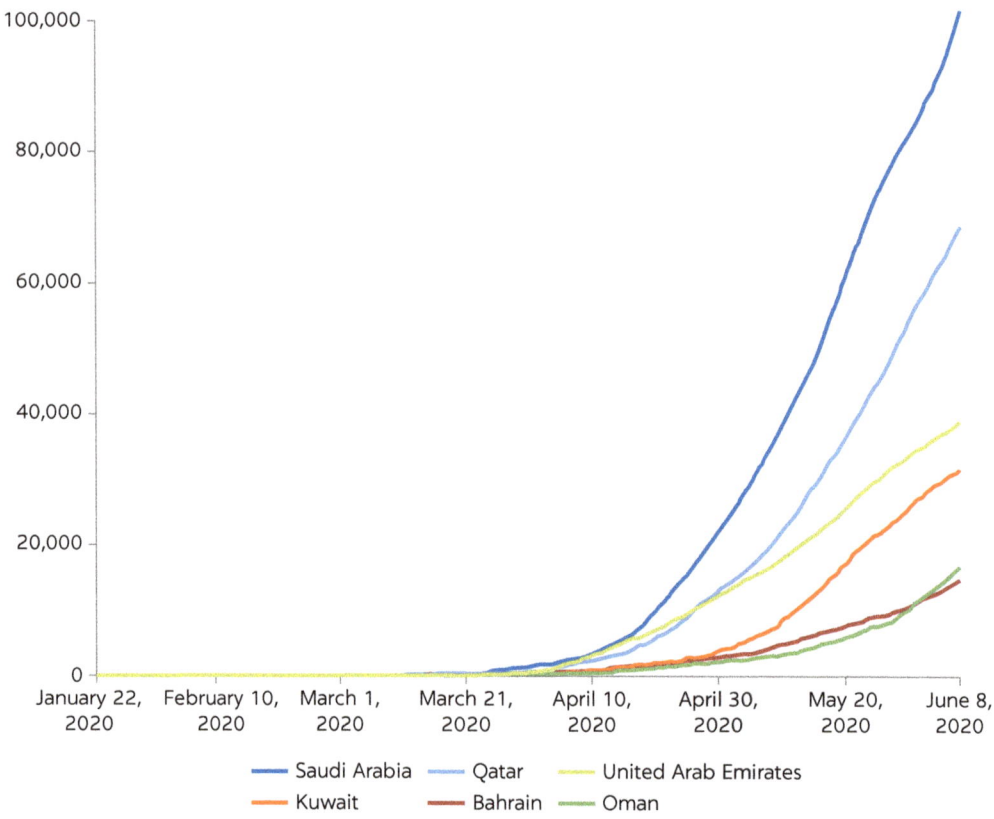

Source: "Coronavirus (COVID-19) Cases." Accessed June 9, 2020, at https://ourworldindata.org/covid-cases?country=KWT+BHR+OMN+QAT+SAU+ARE.
Note: The number of confirmed cases is lower than the number of total cases; the main reason is limited testing.

TABLE 4.1 Status of COVID-19 in the Gulf Cooperation Council countries

COUNTRY	CUMULATIVE CONFIRMED CASES	TOTAL DEATHS	CASE FATALITY RATE (%)	TOTAL RECOVERED	TOTAL TESTS	TOTAL POPULATION	TESTS/1,000 POPULATION
Bahrain	14,763	26	0.18	9,468	367,056	1,696,592	216.35
Kuwait	31,848	264	0.83	20,205	315,285	4,265,955	73.91
Oman	17,486	81	0.46	3,793	111,376	5,096,376	21.85
Qatar	68,790	54	0.08	44,338	255,533	2,807,805	91.01
Saudi Arabia	101,914	712	0.70	72,817	958,237	34,774,012	27.56
United Arab Emirates	38,808	276	0.71	21,806	2,500,000	9,881,840	252.99

Source: COVID-19 CORONAVIRUS PANDEMIC. Worldometer Global COVID-19 data accessed June 8, 2020, at https://www.worldometers.info/coronavirus/#countries.

than 1 percent among those who tested positive (table 4.1). The case fatality rate should, however, be considered with caution because it depends only on the number of cases that tested positive, while the number of infected people may be much higher, and the actual case fatality rate would then be lower.

COVID-19 has caused negative supply and demand shocks, and the oil price drop has hit fiscal revenues hard and weakened external balances—oil accounts for up to 50 percent of the GCC countries' GDP and 90 percent of their export and fiscal revenues. Early action helped limit COVID-19–related deaths. A tough trade-off is envisaged; addressing the impact of COVID-19 will require fiscal stimulus, whereas low oil revenues require fiscal retrenchment. The GCC governments may run down reserves, increase debt, or both, further compromising medium-term recovery prospects, especially in view of multiyear low oil prices. (See "Public Health Considerations for Reopening an Economy" later in this chapter.)

Several GCC countries have provided stimulus measures to support citizens and strengthen businesses. For example, Bahrain unveiled an $11.4 billion package; Kuwait announced a $16.5 billion additional lending facility for small and medium enterprises, in addition to financial measures; Qatar announced a $23 billion package, alongside financial and economic incentives specifically for the private sector; Saudi Arabia announced a $13 billion stimulus effort to support businesses and extend finance to small and medium enterprises; and the United Arab Emirates announced a $27 billion stimulus plan, including additional subsidies for water and electricity for citizens, and for commercial and industrial activities (Economic and Social Commission for Western Asia 2020).

IMPLICATIONS FOR HUMAN CAPITAL

Although the stimulus packages may provide some initial relief, the COVID-19 pandemic may erode human capital, reveal weaknesses in the systems, and exacerbate preexisting vulnerabilities in the region, such as weak health system preparedness, learning gaps, and inequalities. The pandemic may also be an opportunity to accelerate some of the reforms that would have otherwise taken longer to be adopted, such as the use of technology in education and expansion of cash transfers to vulnerable individuals. A "new normal" may need to be considered in which human capital development takes place in a context in which countries are also managing response and recovery efforts; this will mean planning for agile and flexible service delivery, with careful consideration of implications for individuals.

The pandemic has negatively affected health and education systems, the labor market, and social protection. Access to routine health care services has been disrupted and most elective surgeries postponed. One report estimates that some 50 percent of regular care in the GCC is on hold; 400,000 doctors, nurses, dentists, allied health, and other care professionals are not able to practice medicine; and about 8 million patient contacts are cancelled every week (Gupta Strategists 2020). In education, more than 12 million students are not attending schools and universities because of COVID-19–related closures. The technology and mass media measures taken will compensate only in part for students' losses in learning and social interaction with peers and teachers. Similarly, tens of thousands of jobs will be lost, paychecks will shrink, and social benefits will not fully compensate for the loss in income.

One key preexisting vulnerability is the lack of public health readiness in the GCC countries, also a significant challenge globally. The Global Health Security Index (GHSI) is a comprehensive assessment and benchmarking of health security and related capabilities across the 195 countries that make up the states that are parties to the WHO International Health Regulations 2005. The GHSI includes indicators that cover six categories: prevention, detection and reporting, rapid response, health system, compliance with international norms, and risk environment.

TABLE 4.2 **Global Health Security Index and rank of the GCC countries**

GULF COOPERATION COUNCIL COUNTRY	GHSI	RANK
Bahrain	39.4	88
Kuwait	46.1	59
Oman	43.1	73
Qatar	41.2	82
Saudi Arabia	49.3	47
United Arab Emirates	46.7	56

Source: https://www.ghsindex.org/.
Note: GHSI = Global Health Security Index.

The average overall GHSI score is 40.2 out of a possible 100. The index shows that, collectively, international preparedness for epidemics and pandemics remains very weak: 116 high- and middle-income countries, including all the GCC countries (table 4.2), scored lower than 50. The GCC countries' scores range from a low of 39.4 for Bahrain to a high of 49.3 for Saudi Arabia, lower than the average score of 51.9 reported for high-income countries.

Interestingly, however, the GHSI score and ranking do not necessarily translate into action on the ground. The GCC countries' performance in addressing the crisis has been better than what the GHSI would suggest. The United States, for example, which ranked first, with a score of 83.5, was slow in taking early actions and ended up with the highest number of cases worldwide, despite its reported level of preparedness.

Given the interrelationship of public health readiness, rapid response, and the severity of the pandemic, the WHO developed a more specific measure to assess countries' capacity to respond to COVID-19, in line with the global Strategic Preparedness and Response Plan.[2]

The categorization of countries is based on the following:

- *Country preparedness capacity.* A rating of 5 implies the country has high capacity for preventing, detecting, and responding to a public health emergency.
- *Response category.* A rating of 5 corresponds to higher risk, that is, the country has demonstrated community transmission; a rating of 4 indicates localized transmission; a rating of 3 indicates imported cases; 2 indicates there is a risk of imported cases; and 1 is for all other countries.

Based on this measurement, the United Arab Emirates had the highest capacity, with a rating of 5, while the other GCC countries were assessed at category 4. On the response category, all the GCC countries were assessed at level 4, which reflects local transmission, similar to most European and Middle Eastern countries. A key concern is the impact of the crisis on health beyond just its direct impact. The COVID-19 crisis has the potential to overwhelm existing health systems, affecting both emergency and nonemergency specialties. Health workers' capacities and mental well-being could also become stretched. Under typical circumstances, many patients already need the relevant expertise, ventilators or oxygen, and hospital beds, and a further escalation of cases could edge such patients out of care. Moreover, postponing primary care visits and elective surgeries may lead to health complications, all of which can lead to worsening health outcomes and thus affect productivity and human capital.

A primary concern is the well-being of children and young people during this time of significant change to their routines. A short-term negative impact on their ability to continue as normal with their learning is to be expected, both during school closures and on return to school. A lag in learning progress is likely, particularly given that this interruption to schooling has come at a crucial time in the school year, with the buildup to year-end examinations. Where remote learning opportunities are provided without the structure for each child or student to have a direct link to their teachers, progress will vary depending on students' self-study abilities and their parents' ability to understand and guide the learning. For this reason, inequalities are likely to increase, widening gaps that are already large. Those children who struggle with reading, self-regulation, or digital skills are likely to fall further behind and suffer from feelings of isolation and inadequacy; this is particularly the case for those who usually receive support from specialized teachers.

The investments that some GCC countries have already made in education technology (edtech) solutions—including tools that enable teachers to provide materials, set tasks, and conduct virtual classes, and that enable students to upload work and receive feedback—will pay off in the medium to long term. This is particularly true for systems that have developed platforms or portals that provide a clear scope and sequence of curricular materials in accessible and user-friendly modes, for both teachers and students. However, most of the world's education systems (including high-performing ones) are finding that they need to improve the content and rollout of their remote learning provision and of their edtech solutions to cope with a situation in which all students are learning remotely for unknown lengths of time. In the GCC countries, these platforms often require improvements in the underlying curricula and materials, more training for teachers to effectively use them during regular school operations, support for students and parents to effectively navigate and use technology-based solutions, and improvements to internet coverage and connectivity and access to hardware.

Investments in edtech solutions alone will not be sufficient, however. The GCC countries share a common problem of low levels of learning despite high investments in education. For example, between 32 percent and 51 percent of 10-year-olds cannot read and understand a short, age-appropriate text, which will limit their ability to engage with and benefit from remote learning provision.[3] The loss of learning due to COVID-19–related school closures is inevitable, at least in the short term and possibly longer if school closures are extended or occur frequently. For several GCC countries with very low enrollment in early childhood education, and where demand for early childhood education is low, convincing parents of the benefits of sending their children to preschool settings outside the home may become more difficult. Furthermore, the demands of protracted remote learning may impact women's decisions to enter the labor market. All these issues are likely to set back GCC countries' efforts to improve existing low levels of learning and develop the human capital needed to achieve their ambitious "Visions" (appendix A) and to diversify their economies.

Another concern is the dire situation of millions of low-wage foreign workers, whom the GCC countries have come to depend on, but who have lost their jobs and can neither return home nor rely on safety nets for financial support during the crisis.

Foreign labor makes up half or more of the population in many GCC countries, and accounts for high proportions of COVID-19 infections.

Workers experiencing such setbacks and unemployment in the downturn are more likely to experience additional episodes of joblessness and have lower wages in the aftermath of the crisis. Unemployment and hardship can also lead to demoralization, depression, and other psychological traumas, lowering affected individuals' productivity and attractiveness to employers.

MEASURES TAKEN BY THE GCC COUNTRIES

Early investments in health can reduce the need to take costly preventive measures when epidemics strike. For example, the Republic of Korea, Singapore, and Taiwan, China, seem to have benefited from high levels of testing, tracking, and quarantine, although second and even third waves of the COVID-19 pandemic are now hitting these economies, sometimes hard.

The GCC countries undertook sound public health measures based on their experience in combating MERS-CoV in 2012, and other measures, such as suspending passenger flights into and out of the country; imposing lockdowns, introducing curfews, curtailing religious and sports activities, asking many office-based workers to work from home, and closing movie theatres, gyms, public swimming pools, public beaches, and theme parks.

But as in many countries, the poor—mainly low-wage foreign workers, who make up large shares of GCC populations—may bear the brunt of the epidemic (Hubbard 2020). The proportion of nonnationals in the employed population in the GCC countries is 70.4 percent on average, ranging from 56 percent to 93 percent for individual countries.[4] In some GCC countries, elements of the government response did not cover foreign workers (see the country-specific information below).

The following discussions of country actions for health, education, and social protection and jobs are not exhaustive, but are more an attempt to give an idea of individual countries' measures.

Bahrain

Health.[5] After confirming the first COVID-19 case of a traveler from the Islamic Republic of Iran on February 21, Bahrain closed all theaters, gyms, public swimming pools, and theme parks on March 18; ordered the release of hundreds of prisoners on March 21;[6] and designated the Bahrain International Exhibition & Convention Centre as the main testing center for COVID-19 on March 23. On March 24, Bahrain's central bank instructed foreign exchange companies to sterilize local and overseas currencies and ordered closure of all nonessential commercial enterprises beginning March 26. On March 30, the Ministry of Health (MOH), with the Ministry of Interior, set up sample collection stations across Bahrain where teams collected samples through mobile screening units. On March 31, Bahrain's Information and eGovernment Authority released the BeAware Bahrain application on the Apple and Google Play stores. The application uses global positioning system (GPS) location data to alert users about nearby active cases of COVID-19 or locations visited by positive cases of the disease. On April 6, the authority began distributing electronic waterproof wristbands with location tracking to monitor individuals under home quarantine. On April 7, Bahrain suspended the fees levied on the delivery of health services to foreign patients at public health centers; and on

April 8, the government advised people to wear face masks in public. April 9 saw the MOH launch a COVID-19 drive-through testing center at the Bahrain International Exhibition & Convention Centre, as well as suspend the 7 Bahrain dinar medical consultation fee.

Education. All private and public schools, universities, and nurseries were closed on February 25. On March 17, the Ministry of Education (MOE) began televising live virtual classes for eight hours a day covering all grades (online distance learning or home schooling) using the Microsoft Teams application. Classes were also made available on YouTube and the country's existing elearning portal, Edunet, which was launched in 2015. Edunet contains 408,000 digital materials, including 151,000 activities, 60,000 discussions, 74,000 lessons, and 124,000 enrichment selections prepared by teachers between February 23 and April 14. The portal allowed more than 90 percent of third intermediate and secondary students to take part in live Microsoft Teams lessons.[7]

Social protection and jobs. The government unveiled an $11.4 billion stimulus package to support the economy on March 17, and on April 8 announced that it would spend US$570 million to pay the salaries of all Bahraini employees (an estimated 100,000 workers) in the private sector until June, but excluding foreign workers. The Ministry of Labour and Social Development on April 15 issued a circular stressing the responsibility of employers to protect all workers and individuals present in the workplace from coronavirus risk.[8]

Kuwait

Health.[9] The MOH began detailing coronavirus cases on its website (and on television) on February 24. On April 6, a curfew was introduced from 5 pm to 6 am. Work was suspended across all ministries and government institutions, initially for the period April 12–26 and then extended to May 31. All private health clinics and laboratories were also closed. On April 14, it was announced that medical requests for nationals and those exempt from fees could be made through the MOH. On April 13, the MOH announced a partial closure—including international waters, beach houses, farms, and residential areas—banning walking on beaches, walking inside residential areas, and boat rides. It was announced that all nonemergency government offices would be closed at least through April 23, unless otherwise exempted. All public transportation, including taxi services, was suspended, and all mosques, public parks, beaches, and public spaces were closed until further notice.

Education. The government closed all schools, universities, and military colleges beginning March 1, later extending the closure until August 4, followed by a decision to begin the new school year on December 1, 2020. The MOE eLearning team started work on an eLearning plan and, with the Kuwait Foundation for the Advancement of Sciences, is recording lessons for remote learning and plans to launch an eLearning platform, initially for grade 12 and then grade 11, followed by all levels.[10]

Social protection and jobs. The government announced a series of measures, including $16.5 billion in additional lending to small and medium enterprises; the Central Bank of Kuwait cut its lending rate by 100 basis points; lenders were asked to postpone loan repayments in industries affected by the crisis; and capital adequacy requirements were reduced by 2.5 percent. In addition, the government has submitted to parliament a draft law that would allocate 500 million Kuwaiti dinar ($1.6 billion, or 1.4 percent of GDP) to fight the pandemic.[11]

The Public Authority for Manpower upgraded its online services by launching "Khidma As'hal," which provides easier processes for registration and transfer of workers. The Public Authority for Manpower also investigated allegations that some businesses refused to pay their workers' wages.[12] No specific actions have been taken so far to support foreign workers.

Oman

Health.[13] Following confirmation of the first two cases of COVID-19 returning from the Islamic Republic of Iran, the government introduced airport screening for travelers arriving from endemic countries and set in place systems for isolation and surveillance of symptomatic arrivals. On March 3, all retail outlets, including shopping malls and supermarkets, were instructed to install sanitizers. On March 12, the Supreme Committee on Coronavirus set out six decisions, starting March 15 for 30 days, with prohibitions on tourist visas, sports activities, nonclass student activities, and entry of cruise ships, and limiting attendance at court sessions to only those involved in the court cases. On March 18, treatment services provided for routine nonemergency medical cases were temporarily suspended; and on March 17, a ban was imposed on entry of all non-Omanis into the country, with the exception of GCC nationals. On March 19, the MOH launched the Tarassud app on the Apple Store as an interactive COVID-19 map; and on March 22, the Supreme Committee directed government agencies to reduce the number of employees present in the government sector to no more than 30 percent of the total number of employees. On March 25, the Supreme Committee decided to activate the "Medical Response and Public Health" sector and the "Shelter and Relief" sector. Several hospitals, including Al Nahda Hospital, announced the suspension of all outpatient appointments and surgical appointments starting April 1. On April 6, it was announced that some hospitals had initiated community psychological support for anyone needing it. On April 8, the entire capital was placed under lockdown for April 10–22. On April 9, the MOH announced that all COVID-19 tests and treatment would be free for everyone. On April 14, the MOH began using plasma from recovered COVID-19 patients to treat critically ill patients in the Royal Hospital.

Education. The MOE initially ruled out the possibility of closing schools due to coronavirus outbreak fears,[14] but on March 4 called for suspending all events and educational activities at the governorate or school level until further notice.[15] All classes in schools, universities, and other educational institutions were suspended for 30 days beginning March 15. This decision was revised in early April by the Supreme Committee to remain in effect until further notice.[16] The MOE began broadcasting live televised lessons on Oman TV, starting with secondary students, and launched a distance education portal on its website. The MOE is also collaborating with private sector bodies to support educational digital initiatives for teachers, and is partnering with Omantel to provide access to the "G Suite for Education" digital platform for more than 450,000 students in grades 5–12.

Social protection and jobs. Oman's Ministry of Manpower issued guidelines to employers confirming that during these unprecedented times, employers are required to pay staff their wages in full.[17]

Qatar

Health.[18] On February 24, precautionary measures were taken as recommended by the WHO to prepare for COVID-19, including preparing residential buildings for quarantine. On February 25, the Ministry of Public health (MOPH) advised that unnecessary travel to countries with COVID-19 cases should be avoided. On February 27, the first case of COVID-19 was confirmed. On March 10, *shisha* and hookah smoking were banned in cafes and restaurants, and on March 12, people were cautioned to avoid social gatherings. On March 23, the MOPH publicly sought volunteers to support Qatar's response to the COVID-19 outbreak, while launching a volunteer campaign called "For Qatar." Working hours were changed to 7 am to 2 pm on March 25. On March 28, the MOPH activated remote access channels for health care services, and on March 29 nonemergency health services at private health facilities—including dental clinics, dermatology centers, laser clinics, and plastic surgeries—were suspended. Between March 30 and April 8, Hazm Mebaireek General Hospital was designated as the national treatment facility, and two primary health care centers were selected for screening, testing, and quarantining COVID-19 patients. On April 9, the MOPH intensified health control campaigns for food establishments as a precautionary measure. On April 13, the government sought to improve outreach to non-Arabic speakers and issued guidelines for employers and employees in several languages. On April 16, the health sector launched a remote COVID-19 and diabetes outreach program. All workers have access to free testing and health care, regardless of their status.[19]

Education. Beginning March 10, all schools and universities in Qatar were closed until further notice. The Ministry of Education and Higher Education issued a remote learning plan for the 2019/20 school year for grades 1 to 12. Students can follow their lessons remotely via Qatar TV, YouTube, or the ministry's distance learning portal. Daily assessments are available through the Microsoft Teams platform, which teachers can use to deliver their video lessons; weekly assessments for students are available at the end of the last subject's lesson according to the weekly schedule.

Social protection and jobs. The Ministry of Administrative Development, Labour, and Social Affairs launched a 24/7 hotline to receive workers' complaints and feedback in multiple languages. In the first 11 days, the hotline received more than 10,000 calls, including 8,590 from workers and 1,633 from employers.[20] Many enterprises have been exempted from paying rent for several months.[21] In addition, the government announced that employers would pay full salaries to foreign workers in quarantine or under treatment, and the government has set aside funds to support the companies.[22]

Saudi Arabia

Health.[23] All international flights were stopped beginning March 15, followed by domestic flights and on-ground transportation between cities and districts (except for logistics, delivery, and medical services). In a further tightening of restrictions originally launched in late February, on March 20 the government suspended entry and praying by the general public at the Great Mosque in Mecca and the Prophet's Mosque in Medina. Announcements were also made that all prayers were to be conducted at home. The MOH is testing for COVID-19 in densely populated areas. In addition, the government is using some 3,600 currently vacant public school buildings to accommodate low-wage foreign workers from densely populated areas. The MOH also established an e-Health strategy that includes the use of telemedicine.[24] On March 30, the King instructed that all COVID-19 patients should be treated for free.[25] In addition, the MOH mandated that health insurance cards were to be extended automatically for at least six months. The government initiated a "Home Medicine Program" to deliver required medications to patients with chronic diseases.

Education. The MOE is using television and social media to broadcast lessons for all grades and has designated 127 supervisors and teachers to deliver daily lessons in 112 educational subjects through 19 television channels, broadcasting nationally from a classroom in Riyadh.[26] By March 28, 6 million students had started virtual schooling.[27] The Education and Training Evaluation Commission postponed the academic achievement test required for transition to higher education from April 17–21 to May or June using two options: remote testing or paper-based testing.[28] The MOE has cancelled the remainder of the school year and has declared that all students will be promoted to the next grade, while remote learning opportunities will continue.[29] Universities (public and private) put in place remote learning as early as the day after closure. More than 1.2 million users had attended 107,000 learning hours in more than 7,600 virtual classes as of April 4. Options for final university examinations are under consideration.[30]

Social protection and jobs. The government announced a major wage subsidy program for Saudi citizens working in the private sector, covering roughly 60 percent of their wages. The Ministry of Human Resources and Social Development launched a "community fund," with capital of 500 million Saudi Arabian riyals (about $133 million), to support Saudi citizens most affected by the pandemic, including the poor, people with disabilities, prisoners' families, and the elderly.[31] For foreign workers, the monthly dependents' levy was waived and various visa regulations were relaxed, including automatic renewal of expired residencies for three months, correction of illegal status, and a six-month extension for exit and reentry visas for expatriates abroad.[32] Foreign workers were also permitted to work for other employers in an expansion of the "Ajeer" system. Foreign workers can request delays and deferrals for electricity and rent payments. To support firms, the government temporarily suspended the wage protection system.

United Arab Emirates

Health.[33] The Ministry of Health and Prevention stated on March 7 that more than 620 school buildings and 6,000 buses had been sterilized.[34] Dubai started an 11-day sterilization campaign on March 22. In mid-April, the United Arab Emirates was ranked the world's 10th best for the treatment of the coronavirus, according to the Deep Knowledge Group, and the first among Arab nations. The country also continues to ramp up testing services, launching a home testing service for people with disabilities and drive-through centers.[35] The Dubai Police Force has used artificial intelligence solutions to distinguish vehicles that have movement permits or belong to people working within vital sectors from vehicles belonging to individuals in breach of the lockdown that came into force on April 5.[36] Hospitals across the United Arab Emirates have adopted telemedicine services to help patients avoid exposure to the risk of infection and minimize the burden on the health care system.[37] In addition, the Telecommunications Regulatory Authority has launched 18 initiatives to support distance learning and the safety of citizens, residents, and visitors.[38]

Education. Schools and universities closed for four weeks beginning March 8, and as of March 22 virtual classes were launched for schools and universities for two weeks.[39] On March 30, virtual classes were extended until the end of the academic year in June.[40] The MOE has rolled out a remote learning system through its Smart Learning Portal, which was launched in 2012. Initiatives are also under way to ensure continuity of education for vulnerable groups, such as the "Education Uninterrupted" campaign to support distance education for low-income students, launched with Dubai Cares.

Social protection and jobs. The government announced a 1.5 billion Emirati dirham ($408.4 million) stimulus package on March 12 to reduce the cost of doing business and to simplify business procedures, especially in the commercial, retail, external trade, tourism, and energy sectors.[41] Stimulus packages vary by emirate, but at the federal level, a new decree pertaining to foreign workers was issued to encourage firms to consider alternative methods for reducing costs other than by terminating workers. It allows firms to provide foreign workers, subject to mutual agreement, with the alternative of working remotely, of taking paid or unpaid leave, or of taking a temporary or permanent reduction in salary. Firms must also register workers on a job-matching virtual platform and pay them housing and other allowances until they find another job or leave the country. Finally, the government also extended expired residencies and visas until December 2020.

POSSIBLE ADDITIONAL MEASURES

The disruptions caused by the COVID-19 pandemic will have a long-term impact if governments do not taken action to mitigate the effects of the crisis on vulnerable people. Although the GCC countries have announced some measures in this area, successful implementation will be crucial, and monitoring efforts will have to be ramped up. Monitoring efforts have been hindered in the past by low capacity and confidentiality concerns. This crisis may be the opportunity to address those shortcomings.

All the GCC governments should continue to invest in strengthening their health systems. Doing so is critical for breaking the chains of transmission and for diagnosing and treating cases while maintaining essential services. Protecting the health of frontline health workers is equally important, as are anticipating and addressing the mental health needs of the health workforce. Finally, continuing to assess and mitigate potential financial barriers to accessing care related to COVID-19—but also other essential health services, including for the foreign population—is critical, in line with the need to assess and mitigate potential physical access barriers for vulnerable groups, and to mitigate impacts on household financial security, productivity, and human capital.

Additional mitigating policy measures include, as a priority, supporting the many foreign workers in the GCC region. GCC nationals are well protected through various safety nets when they lose work, but low-wage foreign workers have no access to such programs. The main social benefit they have access to—the end-of-service benefit—is not very effective at the moment: low-wage foreign workers are not necessarily fired, but their hours are reduced and their pay is suspended; and even when they are laid off, liquidity constraints might prevent companies from paying end-of-service benefits. At the same time, because returning to their home countries is not an option, many of them are stranded in the GCC countries without proper support. Wage subsidy programs and new safety net programs can help provide support to this vulnerable population while ensuring that they can rejoin their companies quickly after the end of the crisis. Wage subsidy programs can also support firms in retaining already-trained workers and, therefore, in lowering their costs of rehiring once the crisis is over. In this way, such programs may prevent productive firms from going out of business and thereby speed up economic recovery.

To understand and tackle the likely widening learning gaps—whereby students from more advantaged backgrounds are more readily able to access and engage with remote learning opportunities—countries should consider implementing rapid telephone surveys of teachers and parents to gauge students' engagement with remote learning provision and teachers' and parents' ability to support students' learning. Once schools reopen, teachers will need to be able to assess each student's learning level and education needs, keeping in mind that children in the same class could have been through very different learning experiences during the school shutdown. Targeted remedial support will be crucial for bringing lagging students up to speed.

Efforts should be made to accelerate the availability and use of edtech and upgrade its content to support—but not replace—classroom teaching. These efforts will help build system resilience so that any future requirement for remote learning results in a smoother transition, and should include protocols and procedures for future disruptions, which may become part of the "new normal."

Furthermore, existing social safety net programs for GCC nationals could be extended to cover freelance workers such as the self-employed and platform workers. Currently, safety nets are geared toward supporting certain categories of beneficiaries, including the disabled, widows, and the elderly. Freelance workers are at risk of falling through the cracks because they do not belong to any of these groups, although they are in much need of support. Quick changes to the eligibility criteria for these programs can help close these gaps.

The COVID-19 crisis underscores the importance of integrated social protection delivery systems for reaching the most vulnerable segments of the population. Countries that have invested in developing such systems can better cope with the adverse effects of the crisis by delivering immediate cash to cover basic needs.

To understand the financial impact on households and employers, governments should also consider implementing quick response surveys online or via telephone targeted to citizens and foreign households and firms. The timely collection of data allows governments to react quickly to the crisis. Governments can, for example, track the impact of changing prices and employment losses on households and their coping strategies or, for firms, the financial impact and mitigating measures taken, such as layoffs, provision of unpaid leave, or salary cuts.

In summary, key strategies already under way in the GCC countries for developing human capital may need to be accelerated and honed to overcome the shocks caused by COVID-19.

PUBLIC HEALTH CONSIDERATIONS FOR REOPENING AN ECONOMY

The stringent measures taken by the governments of the GCC countries to flatten the pandemic curve have led to the shutting down of many economic activities. Because there is a trade-off between the need to curb the pandemic and the need to reopen the economy, policy makers are contemplating the question of when to start reopening and in which sectors. Many reports and articles have attempted to answer this question, mostly for high-income countries, and offer different—but converging—approaches.

The American Enterprise Institute, working with Johns Hopkins University, proposes a four-phase stepwise approach, depending on the ability to aggregate and analyze data in real time (American Enterprise Institute 2020): *Phase I: Slow the spread.* This is the current phase in which community transmission is occurring and most activities are shut down. These measures will need to be in place until transmission has measurably slowed and health infrastructure can be scaled up to safely manage the outbreak and care for the sick. *Phase II: Gradual reopening.* This phase can be launched when the health system is able to safely diagnose, treat, and isolate COVID-19 cases and their contacts. However, some physical distancing measures and limitations on gatherings will still need to be in place to prevent transmission from accelerating again. *Phase III: Establish immune protection and lift physical distancing.* In Phase III, physical distancing restrictions and other Phase II measures can be lifted when safe and effective tools for mitigating the risk of COVID-19 are available, including broad surveillance, therapeutics that can rescue patients with significant disease or prevent serious illness in those most at risk, or a safe and effective vaccine. *Phase IV: Rebuild readiness for the next pandemic.* This phase will require investment in research and development initiatives, expansion of the public health and health care infrastructure and workforce, and clear governance structures to execute strong preparedness plans.

Vital Strategies, an international public health consultancy, proposes an "adaptive approach" consisting of four stages: preparedness, containment, mitigation, and suppression.[42] Containment involves preventing the spread of disease in early stages of transmission (sporadic and clusters of cases) through measures such as early detection and isolation of cases and contact tracing and quarantine. Mitigation consists of minimizing the epidemic impact from local and widespread transmission, delaying the outbreak peak, and reducing the peak number of cases to reduce strain on the health care system, achieved largely through public health social measures and specific treatments, when available. Suppression entails reducing and maintaining low levels of disease transmission through intermittent loosening and tightening of public health social measures, detection and isolation of cases, and contact tracing and quarantine.

These two strategies offer a public health approach based on slowing transmission and strengthening public health capacity in which countries progressively relax measures as new cases slow and public health capacity increases.

Other reports have combined public health considerations with economic considerations. For example, McKinsey proposes a matrix that determines the extent of the health care system's ability to handle virus transmission along two dimensions.[43] First is virus spread, which consists of the number of new daily infections, the virus transmission rate, and new daily cases requiring hospitalization and treatment in an intensive care unit. Second is public health readiness, which requires medical capacity to manage critical cases, adequate medical resources, the ability to rapidly test, and effectiveness in tracking and isolation. In addition, the approach analyzes the prioritization of reopening economic sectors based on two dimensions: the risk of virus transmission in these sectors, and their economic relevance.

Brookings offers a variant of this view, emphasizing virus-proofing public nodes, especially airports and rail stations, with a focus on telework and protecting leading industry clusters and "Main Street."[44]

The international consultancy Castalia presents a risk-cost framework that weighs the epidemic risks of lifting measures against the economic costs of maintaining them.[45] For New Zealand, it suggests lifting domestic travel restrictions as soon as possible (and international ones much later), easing compulsory shutdowns when the virus reproductive rate is low enough, and keeping in place restrictions on large gatherings. It also proposes keeping in place intensified private and public hygiene, as well as heightened surveillance, for a longer period.

A paper from the United Kingdom by Lyons and Ormerod suggests a similar risk-calibrated approach based on "traffic lights," where red represents limited openings and high individual vigilance; orange expanded openings and continued individual caution; and green going back to (a new) normal.[46]

This growing literature suggests considerable agreement about the key steps toward reopening, particularly the importance of seeing declining rates of infection, strengthened public health responses, and increasingly granular data about epidemic transmission dynamics and intervention impacts to help determine which sectors of the economy can be gradually reopened.

Where widespread lockdowns have been instituted because of community transmission, striking the right balance between the health costs and the economic costs is a priority and will require countries to take a carefully calibrated approach to easing lockdowns as soon as the disease situation allows. Recognizing the many uncertainties surrounding COVID-19, and based on current knowledge, there are some key considerations for easing lockdowns (World Bank 2020). For the GCC countries, the following are the four key public health considerations for reopening the economy.

Epidemic force

The greater the epidemic force, the more urgent, large-scale, and long-lasting the required lockdowns, and the greater the likelihood and size of subsequent rebounds when measures are relaxed. The overall epidemic force is primarily about contagiousness, called the reproduction rate, and is about 2–2.5—double that of influenza. It is important to drive this rate to less than 1 to reopen safely. Other causes of epidemic force are "superspreading" events, such as religious gatherings and festivals, and, more permanently, homes for the aged and hospitals. A key element of epidemic force is community transmission, where the virus spreads locally without imported infection chains. Epidemic force also influences the likelihood and size of further epidemic waves, because unless the reproduction rate is driven to less than 1 before measures are relaxed, rapid, large rebounds are likely and even subsequent epidemic waves are still likely, though they may be slower and smaller.

In the GCC countries, the large expatriate population and international travel hubs in some countries were enlarging the epidemic force, given that most of the new cases were imported or traced to imported cases before local transmission began. This risk was mitigated by the capacity to implement targeted measures, such as protecting the borders to control imported infections, quarantining suspected cases, and cancellation of major public gatherings to limit community transmission. These measures can lay the groundwork for reopening internally.

Population health

The larger the pool of the elderly, the comorbid, and health workers, and the higher the number of these groups infected, the less a country may contemplate reopening. Coronavirus fatality can be as high as 10 percent among tested cases when those infected are elderly, comorbid (including those with lung, heart, or liver disease or with diabetes, as well as the obese, hypertensive, immunocompromised, and smokers), or health workers (who may be exposed to repeated, high viral doses). Air pollution, housing density, and malnutrition may also exacerbate disease progression. In contrast, case fatality can be les than 0.5 percent in healthy young communities with good health services.

In the GCC countries, prevalence of noncommunicable diseases, such as diabetes, and their risk factors, such as obesity, among nationals will be a serious challenge, which may be offset by the large, relatively young expatriate population, although the living conditions of low-wage foreign workers are often accelerating cluster transmission, but of less critical cases. The GCC countries need to do far more about the teeming environments in which millions of low-wage foreign workers live and work (*Economist* 2020).

Public health and health services capacity

Countries with high and tested public health capacity have experienced fewer infections because they have managed to prevent imported infections from becoming community transmission and thus they can reopen earlier—Germany, for example. If countries do not possess these core pandemic capabilities, they must use the time bought by lockdowns to rapidly strengthen these functions because they will be required for reopening. The core public health skills are the ability to protect and screen effectively at borders; test, isolate, and treat positives; trace contacts; quarantine the exposed; and minimize unlinked cases (those without identifiable contact chains). For example, Bahrain flattened the pandemic curve through its strong public health measures. In addition, a country needs well-protected health workers and safe health facilities before it can consider reopening its economy. Adequate hospital and critical care beds also increase a country's confidence in its ability to reopen.

Health service capacity, particularly at hospitals, is of paramount importance. The first imperative is effective personal protective equipment for all health workers so as to avoid multiple consequences: their becoming infected, hospitals superspreading infection concentrators, and health workers rapidly becoming overwhelmed by repeated, intensive viral doses and then sickening and dying quickly—in turn overwhelming health systems and causing higher mortality among patients. Other necessities include effective isolation wards and enough critical care places, equipment, and supplies, including oxygen concentrators and ventilators, and critical care teams.

Health services in the GCC countries have effectively managed the case load, as reflected by the low case fatality rate, which remains below 1 percent among those tested positive. However, given that cases are set to increase in some GCC countries, governments will want to pay more attention to ensuring the readiness of their health services to manage critical cases.

Scientific and technological innovations

The results of scientific efforts have been quite impressive and offer the hope of a relatively rapid pathway to reopening. Their impact is generally seen in four broad categories: digital mobility and public health tracking tools, testing, treatment, and vaccines. The first and second are the most relevant for the GCC countries, and the last would indeed be transformative.

There are two types of tests that can help governments shorten and soften economically costly suppression measures while still containing the COVID-19 pandemic. The first—a polymerase chain reaction assay—identifies people currently infected by testing for the presence of the live virus in the subject, which can help contain the disease because it facilitates the identification of infected persons. The second—an antibody test—identifies those rendered immune after being infected by searching for COVID-19–specific antibodies, which can help assess the extent of immunity in the general population or subgroups, to fine-tune social isolation (de Walque and others 2020).

The fruits of digital mobility and public health tracking tools are already being harvested. COVID-19 is the most digitally tracked pandemic in history, with lockdowns accompanied by almost instant digital mobility and distancing measures fed into mathematical models that are updated and recalibrated daily. Several other digital mobility dashboards complement these reports. It has never been possible to monitor social interventions more precisely or rapidly. Yet the ability to capitalize on these data requires national decision-making capacity and coordination across many different government branches, far beyond the health sector.

As detailed earlier, the United Arab Emirates has used artificial intelligence solutions to monitor compliance with the lockdown, and hospitals have used telemedicine services to reduce the burden on the health care system.

FINAL THOUGHTS

The unprecedented crisis brought about by the pandemic has been the biggest blow to the world economy possibly since the Great Depression of the early 1930s—alongside devastating human capital impacts affecting health, education, and jobs. The GCC countries have taken multiple and often strict measures to protect their populations' health and their economies, often being compelled to make an unavoidable trade-off. As of this writing, however, in early June 2020, these measures appear to be paying off by controlling imported cases but not yet local transmission, which continues to rise, and the epidemic curve is not yet flattening. A GCC country's decision to reopen its economy needs to be based on a close evaluation of the public health considerations to avoid a resurgence of infections and any further erosion of its human capital. Such a decision needs to also bear in mind the wider context of steps taken by other GCC countries—and beyond.

NOTES

1. "COVID-19 Dashboard by the Center for Systems Science and Engineering (CSSE) at Johns Hopkins University (JHU)." https://coronavirus.jhu.edu/map.html.
2. WHO, "Updated Country Preparedness and Response Status for COVID-19 as of 16 March 2020." Accessed at https://www.who.int/who-documents-detail/updated-country-preparedness-and-response-status-for-covid-19-as-of-16-march-2020.
3. "Brief. October 15, 2019. Learning Poverty." https://www.worldbank.org/en/topic/education/brief/learning-poverty.
4. "Labour Migration." https://www.ilo.org/beirut/areasofwork/labour-migration/lang--en/index.htm.
5. Source for this section: "COVID-19 Pandemic in Bahrain." https://en.wikipedia.org/wiki/2020_coronavirus_pandemic_in_Bahrain, unless otherwise stated; accessed April 16, 2020.
6. "Coronavirus: Bahrain One of First Nations to Ease Lockdown as Malls Reopen." https://english.alarabiya.net/en/News/gulf/2020/04/09/Coronavirus-Bahrain-malls-reopen-one-of-the-first-countries-to-loosen-restrictions.
7. "Undersecretary: 'Teams' Online Classes Successful." https://www.bna.bh/en/UndersecretaryTeamsonlineclassessuccessful.aspx?cms=q8FmFJgiscL2fwIzON1%2bDoI1pZFI6zGGH2lJaPHOE5c%3d.
8. "Bahrain: COVID-19 Precautionary Guidelines for Labour Camps Issued." https://www.gulf-insider.com/bahrain-COVID-19-precautionary-guidelines-for-labour-camps-issued/.
9. Source for this section: "COVID-19 Pandemic in Kuwait." https://en.wikipedia.org/wiki/2020_coronavirus_pandemic_in_Kuwait, unless otherwise stated; accessed April 16, 2020.
10. "KFAS Academy Announces Free Online Courses for the Duration of School Closure." http://kfas.com/media/News/NewsDetail?id=6ac10b0f-3ca0-4277-a608-10179470c515#secContent/.
11. "Policy Responses to COVID-19." https://www.imf.org/en/Topics/imf-and-covid19/Policy-Responses-to-COVID-19#K/.
12. "COVID-19 and the World of Work: Country Policy Responses." https://www.ilo.org/global/topics/coronavirus/country-responses/lang--en/index.htm#KW.
13. Source for this section: "COVID-19 Pandemic in Oman." https://en.wikipedia.org/wiki/2020_coronavirus_pandemic_in_Oman, unless otherwise stated; accessed April 16, 2020.
14. "Coronavirus: No Plans to Close Schools in Oman, Says Ministry of Education." https://timesofoman.com/article/2815912/Oman/Education/Coronavirus-No-plans-to-close-schools-in-Oman-says-Ministry-of-Education.

15. "Coronavirus: Ministry of Education Issues Circular to Schools in Oman." https://timesofoman.com/article/2851789/oman/education/coronavirus-ministry-of-education-issues-circular-to-schools-in-oman/.
16. "Oman Suspends Study at All Educational Institutions." https://timesofoman.com/article/2907980/oman/education/oman-suspends-study-at-all-educational-institutions/.
17. "Covid-19: Employment Update—Issues to Consider in Oman." https://www.trowers.com/insights/2020/april/COVID-19---employment-update---issues-to-consider-in-oman.
18. Source for this section: "COVID-19 Pandemic in Qatar." https://en.wikipedia.org/wiki/2020_coronavirus_pandemic_in_Qatar, unless otherwise stated; accessed April 16, 2020.
19. "COVID-19 and the World of Work: Country Policy Responses." https://www.ilo.org/global/topics/coronavirus/country-responses/lang--en/index.htm#QA.
20. "COVID-19 and the World of Work: Country Policy Responses." https://www.ilo.org/global/topics/coronavirus/country-responses/lang--en/index.htm#QA.
21. "COVID-19 and the World of Work: Country Policy Responses." https://www.ilo.org/global/topics/coronavirus/country-responses/lang--en/index.htm#QA.
22. "Qatar to Pay Workers in Quarantine Full Salaries." https://www.aljazeera.com/news/2020/04/qatar-pay-workers-quarantine-full-salaries-200401110548709.html.
23. Source for this section: "COVID-19 Pandemic in Saudi Arabia." https://en.wikipedia.org/wiki/2020_coronavirus_pandemic_in_Saudi_Arabia, unless otherwise stated; accessed April 16, 2020.
24. "COVID-19: Opportunity & Innovation in the Technology Sector in Times of Crisis—A Middle East Perspective." https://www.twobirds.com/en/news/articles/2020/uae/COVID-19-opportunity-and-innovation-in-the-technology-sector-in-times-of-crisis.
25. "Al-Rabiah: By Order of the King, All COVID-19 Patients Will Be Treated for Free." https://www.moh.gov.sa/en/Ministry/MediaCenter/News/Pages/News-2020-03-30-005.aspx.
26. "Topics." https://www.worldbank.org/en/topic/edutech/brief/how-countries-are-using-edtech-to-support-remote-learning-during-the-COVID-19-pandemic.
27. "Saudi Education Ministry Takes on Distance Learning of 6 Million Students in 10 Days." https://www.arabnews.com/node/1648561/saudi-arabia.
28. ETEC social media, April 6, 2020.
29. "Saudi Education Ministry Says Students of All Grades Will Progress to Next Year." https://www.arabnews.com/node/1659976/saudi-arabia.
30. MOE social media, April 4, 2020.
31. "COVID-19 and the World of Work: Country Policy Responses." https://www.ilo.org/global/topics/coronavirus/country-responses/lang--en/index.htm#SA.
32. "Saudi Extends Exit, Re-entry Visas of Expatriates." https://gulfbusiness.com/saudi-extends-exit-re-entry-visas-of-expatriates/.
33. Source for this section: "COVID-19 Pandemic in the United Arab Emirates." https://en.wikipedia.org/wiki/2020_coronavirus_pandemic_in_the_United_Arab_Emirates, unless otherwise stated; accessed April 16, 2020.
34. "Middle East Coronavirus—First Death in Egypt and Bahrain F1 to Take Place without Spectators." https://www.arabnews.com/node/1638396/middle-east.
35. "Coronavirus: UAE Ranks among Top 10 Countries in Treatment Efficacy." https://www.gulf-insider.com/coronavirus-uae-ranks-among-top-10-countries-in-treatment-efficacy/.
36. "COVID-19 Precaution: Dubai Police Using AI to Find Out If Your Trip Was Essential." https://gulfnews.com/uae/COVID-19-precaution-dubai-police-using-ai-to-find-out-if-your-trip-was-essential-1.70829268.
37. "COVID-19: Opportunity & Innovation in the Technology Sector in Times of Crisis—A Middle East Perspective." https://www.twobirds.com/en/news/articles/2020/uae/COVID-19-opportunity-and-innovation-in-the-technology-sector-in-times-of-crisis.
38. "TRA Initiatives in Response to Covid-19." https://www.tra.gov.ae/en/about-tra/tra-initiatives-in-response-to-covid-19.aspx.
39. "Study Online and Stay ahead of the Game." https://gulfnews.com/uae/education/study-online-and-stay-ahead-of-the-game-1.1584015954437.
40. "Coronavirus: UAE Extends Distance Learning till End of School Year." https://english.alarabiya.net/en/News/gulf/2020/03/30/Coronavirus-UAE-extends-distance-learning-till-end-of-school-year.

41. "Dubai Announces AED 1.5 Billion Economic Stimulus Package." https://www.dubai92.com/trending/uae/dubai-announces-aed-1-5-billion-economic-stimulus-package/.
42. "COVID-19 Playbook." https://preventepidemics.org/coronavirus/playbook/.
43. "Covid-19 Briefing Materials: Global Health and Crisis Response." Updated April 13, 2020. https://www.mckinsey.com/~/media/mckinsey/business%20functions/risk/our%20insights/covid%2019%20implications%20for%20business/covid%2019%20april%2013/COVID-19-facts-and-insights-april-13.ashx.
44. "How Our Cities Can Reopen after the COVID-19 Pandemic." https://www.brookings.edu/blog/the-avenue/2020/03/24/how-our-cities-can-reopen-after-the-COVID-19-pandemic/.
45. "After the Lockdown." https://castalia-advisors.com/blog-after-the-lockdown/.
46. "The Traffic-Light Route to Ending the Economic Lockdown." http://www.algorithmiceconomics.com/wp-content/uploads/2020/04/ending_lockdown.pdf.

REFERENCES

American Enterprise Institute. 2020. "National Coronavirus Response: A Road Map to Reopening." Washington, DC. https://www.aei.org/research-products/report/national-coronavirus-response-a-road-map-to-reopening/.

de Walque, Damien, Jed Friedman, Roberta Gatti, and Aaditya Mattoo. 2020. "How Two Tests Can Help Contain COVID-19 and Revive the Economy." Research & Policy Briefs from the World Bank Malaysia Knowledge Hub, No. 29, April 8. http://documents.worldbank.org/curated/en/766471586360658318/pdf/How-Two-Tests-Can-Help-Contain-COVID-19-and-Revive-the-Economy.pdf.

Economic and Social Commission for Western Asia. 2020. "COVID-19: Economic Cost to the Arab Region." Beirut. https://www.unescwa.org/sites/www.unescwa.org/files/escwa-COVID-19-economic-cost-arab-region-en.pdf.

Economist. 2020. "Migrant Workers in Cramped Gulf Dorms Fear Infection." April 23, 2020. https://www.economist.com/middle-east-and-africa/2020/04/23/migrant-workers-in-cramped-gulf-dorms-fear-infection.

Gupta Strategists. 2020. "COVID-19 Pandemic Puts Heavy Pressure on Regular Care Delivery." https://gupta-strategists.nl/storage/files/200326-GS-GCC-Corona-Study-VFinal.pdf.

Hubbard, Ben. 2020. "Coronavirus Fears Terrify and Impoverish Migrants in the Persian Gulf." *New York Times*, April 13, 2020. https://www.nytimes.com/2020/04/13/world/middleeast/persian-gulf-migrants-coronavirus.html.

World Bank. 2020. "Policy Response to COVID-19." Washington, DC.

5 Conclusion

Economic growth depends on human capital, physical capital, and factors affecting the productivity of both. Focusing on human capital, this report draws on the World Bank's Human Capital Project and the Human Capital Index (HCI), which measures the amount of human capital accumulated over a lifetime. The HCI has three components—survival to age 5, learning-adjusted years of school, and health—that are combined to reflect their contribution to worker productivity. The report presents the scores for the Gulf Cooperation Council (GCC) countries on the HCI relative to comparable countries. Though showing wide variation and being higher than the MENA average, the GCC country scores are lower than those in their economic peers—such as Germany, the Republic of Korea, and Singapore—and on par with those in less wealthy nations, such as Mexico, Thailand, and Turkey.

However, the HCI stops at the end of school at age 18 and does not consider postsecondary education or beyond. Therefore, GCC countries need to consider factors in human capital beyond those measured by the HCI through a lifelong approach to human capital formation, at all ages of the life cycle, in a "whole-of-government" approach across sectors. This approach is critical because the income from the oil and gas bounty will not last forever, and because the nature of work has evolved in response to rapid technological change, demanding new skill sets.

The four main challenges for human capital formation in the GCC countries are the following:

- *Low levels of basic proficiency among schoolchildren.* Even with heavy public investment in education, all six GCC countries score lower than other high-income countries on international assessments. Moreover, although school enrollment rates are high, when adjusted for the quality of education, effective educational attainment in the GCC countries is low. Also, boys consistently underperform girls.
- *The mismatch between education and the labor market.* The subjects taught in school do not adequately prepare students with the skills needed for employment.
- *The relatively high rate of adult mortality and morbidity.* Mortality due to noncommunicable diseases, for example, is 71.5 percent, which is very high.

- *The unique labor market.* Wages in the public sector are more generous than those in the private sector (where most new jobs need to be created), and government employment for nationals is almost guaranteed.

To tackle these challenges, the report outlines four strategies for the GCC governments' consideration:

- *Invest in high-quality early childhood development.* This investment will allow the GCC countries to improve the lifelong productivity of its people. Studies have shown that investment in early childhood education pays off handsomely.
- *Prepare youth for the future.* Youth need to be prepared for the future by improving learning outcomes, responding to labor market needs, and reducing health risk factors.
- *Enable greater adult labor force participation.* Adult labor force participation can be expanded by promoting lifelong learning, improving conditions for female labor force participation, providing retraining or upskilling for adults who are unemployed or underemployed, and improving health conditions to reduce adult mortality and morbidity.
- *Create an enabling environment for human capital formation.* Such an environment will enable the GCC countries to increase value for money in public spending on education and health, move toward a multisectoral approach to human capital, and foster shared social and political interests that will lead to greater productivity and prosperity.

These strategies—which the GCC countries will be in a position to take up once the COVID-19 pandemic has run its course and life begins to approach a "new normal"—are based on best practices and evidence from implementation in other countries and feature, in part, some of the six countries' plans for developing their workforces, including their national "Visions" to take their economies and societies further into the twenty-first century.

The GCC countries can achieve—by adopting and then tailoring these strategies—diversified and sustainable growth that does not depend on hydrocarbons. Continued political will, however, is vital in all these endeavors.

APPENDIX A

Government Visions for Accelerating Human Capital Formation

The Gulf Cooperation Council (GCC) countries have developed ambitious "Vision" programs to improve human capital. These programs aspire to build the human capital needed to achieve the goal of economic diversification and sustainability. The GCC countries also have the advantage of possessing the financial resources to allocate significant funds to social sectors and carry out their human development plans. In addition, three GCC countries—Kuwait, Saudi Arabia, and the United Arab Emirates—have been among the first 28 countries to adopt the World Bank's Human Capital Project, signaling their commitment to improving their human capital outcomes. More recently, Bahrain expressed interest in joining the project.

BAHRAIN VISION 2030

The Economic Vision 2030 for Bahrain aims to ensure that every Bahraini has the means to live a secure and fulfilling life and reach his or her full potential, following the principles of sustainability, competitiveness, and fairness.[1] The Vision focuses on economic strategies, the ultimate aim of which is to ensure that every Bahraini household has at least twice as much disposable income in real terms by 2030. The Vision discusses human capital under the principles of sustainability and fairness from both the government and societal perspectives.

Bahrain's goal of sustainability is achievable through improvements in human capital, specifically in education and training in fields such as applied sciences. The goal of fairness seeks to provide equal access to education and health care services, especially by offering job training and reinforcing support for a social safety net.

The development of human capital will enable Bahrain to become more efficient by improving government policies in crucial areas such as the economy, finance, health care, education, the environment, security, and social justice. For example, to create a sustainable financial environment through human capital, the government will invest its oil revenues for future generations while using recurrent revenue that is independent of oil for its daily expenditures. In this way, the government will strengthen its education and health care and build an attractive living and business environment.

Bahrain's economic vision includes three human capital strategies: social assistance, health care, and education:

- *Social assistance.* The government of Bahrain will reward hard work and talent, and it will provide equal access to services. Initiatives include targeting housing support and subsidies to those most in need, supporting and developing talented youths throughout the course of their education, and encouraging private philanthropy and other support for charitable causes. A potential measure of success is the share of households earning above the national minimum income.
- *Health care.* All Bahraini nationals and residents will have access to affordable, high-quality health care. Moreover, they will have a choice between public and private providers that meet international health care standards. In these ways, the government seeks to address the needs of the growing and aging population, as well as of those at risk. The government's plan for improving the health care system would include the following levers: promoting and encouraging a healthy lifestyle; providing quick, easy, and equitable access to high-quality health care; ensuring regulation of the health care system by an independent health regulator; and developing, attracting, and retaining health care talent, and fostering a high-performance ethic among all health care employees. Potential measures of success include greater life expectancy and improvements in provider performance according to health care regulatory standards.
- *Education.* The Vision aims to build a first-rate education system that provides every citizen with educational opportunities appropriate for their individual needs, aspirations, and abilities. Education and training should be relevant to the requirements of Bahrain and its economy, delivered to the highest possible quality standards, and accessible based on ability and merit. The strategies to raise the quality of education include improving teacher recruitment and training, enhancing the management of teacher performance, enhancing teachers' image in society, and increasing the attractiveness of teaching careers; providing high-quality training in the applied and advanced skills required for global competitiveness and attracting new industries to Bahrain; setting standards for high-quality across the education sector, regularly reviewing the performance of educational and training institutions, and comparing them with those of Bahrain's competitors; and encouraging research and development in universities to create the platform for a knowledge-based economy. Potential measures of success include the improvement of educational institutions in independent quality reviews and national examinations, as well as improved scores in international tests of school performance.

NEW KUWAIT VISION 2035

The goal of New Kuwait is "to transform Kuwait into a financial and trade hub, attractive to investors, where the private sector leads the economy, creating competition and promoting production efficiency, under the umbrella of enabling government institutions, which accentuates values, safeguards social identify, and achieves human resource development as well as balanced development, providing adequate infrastructure, advanced legislation and inspiring business environment."[2]

Three out of the seven pillars of the New Kuwait Vision 2035 include components for improving human capital outcomes:

- *Creative human capital.* This pillar aims to reform the education system to better prepare youth to become competitive and productive members of the workforce. The following programs in this pillar involve 27 projects:
    - The improvement of the quality of education
    - The increase of enrollment capacity for higher education
    - The improvement of safety and security systems
    - The support and empowerment of youth
    - The redress of labor market imbalances
    - The care for and integration of persons with disabilities
    - The improvement of care services for the elderly
    - The strengthening of social cohesion
- *High-quality health care.* This pillar aims to improve service quality in the public health care system and to develop national capabilities at a reasonable cost. This pillar includes the following programs, with 19 projects:
    - The improvement of the quality of health services
    - The mitigation of chronic noncommunicable diseases
    - The increase of bed capacity in hospitals
- *Sustainable living environment.* This pillar aims to ensure the availability of living accommodation through environmentally sound resources and tactics. It has 16 projects under different programs, but the most pertinent to human capital is the maintenance of air quality.

OMAN VISION 2040

Of the 12 national priorities in Oman's Vision 2040, 4 directly aim to enhance human capital:[3]

- *Health.* This pillar aims to deliver world-class health services to all citizens and residents of Oman and build a healthy society free of health risks and hazards. The health care plan emphasizes inclusiveness, equity, full coverage of all Omani governorates, and a partnership between government, the private sector, and civil society. In particular, the health plan includes providing high-quality preventive and clinical health care across all levels; building a decentralized health care system operating with quality, transparency, fairness, and accountability; following international best practices in accreditation of medical services, health care centers, laboratories, and medical professionals; diversifying and sustaining the funding sources for the health care system; developing scientific research and innovation in health care by qualified national talent; developing technology-driven medical systems and services, especially using technology to overcome geographic and distance barriers; developing medical specialties and incorporating specialized medical institutes and universities into health coverage; and raising public health awareness in communities that health is a responsibility of all.
- *Education, learning, scientific research, and national capabilities.* The education pillar aims to create a knowledge-based society and develop competitive national talent through inclusive education, lifelong learning, and scientific research. The education plan revolves around two aspects. The first focuses on improving the quality of basic and higher education through the

development of educational institutions, faculty, and staff; the application of international standards for accreditation; the use of modern teaching and learning techniques; and the incorporation of Islamic principles and Omani values and identity. The second focuses on developing scientific and educational curricula, which can be achieved by diversifying and sustaining funding for applied scientific research, promoting innovation in various fields, and strengthening partnerships between research institutions and the private sector.

- *Labor market and employment.* This pillar aims to build a dynamic labor market that attracts talent and keeps up with demographic, economic, knowledge, and technological changes. The labor plan includes developing a skilled and productive workforce and a positive work culture; building labor administration based on efficiency, productivity, and innovation, for example, through qualifications, promotions, and incentives; attracting and recruiting a technical and skilled workforce (from abroad); and establishing labor laws and regulations to promote professional standards and to encourage a stimulating and dynamic work environment.
- *Welfare and social protection.* The social protection pillar will provide a decent and sustainable life for all and empower women, children, youth, persons with disabilities, and the most vulnerable groups. The social protection plan includes establishing an effective, sustainable, and fair social safety network; integrating social protection, targeting the most vulnerable groups and empowering them to be self-dependent and contributors to the national economy; advancing social services and programs, community social responsibility programs, civic voluntary contributions, and socioeconomic empowerment programs targeting women and youth; developing effective partnerships between the government, the private sector, and civil society; and encouraging sports activities.

QATAR NATIONAL VISION 2030

Qatar's National Vision (QNV) 2030 aims for Qatar to become an advanced society capable of sustaining its development and providing a high standard of living for its people.[4] QNV 2030 defines the long-term goals for the country and provides a framework within which national strategies and implementation plans can be developed.

Human capital is one of the four interconnected pillars of sustainable development in QNV 2030. According to the Qatar National Development Strategy 2018–2022,[5] human development focuses on the following three areas:

- *Education and high-quality training.* Qatar aims to build a modern world-class educational system that provides students with a first-rate education, comparable to that offered anywhere in the world. The system will provide citizens with excellent training and opportunities to develop to their full potential, preparing them for success in a changing world with increasingly complex technical requirements. The system will also encourage analytical and critical thinking, as well as creativity and innovation. It will promote social cohesion and respect for Qatari society's values and heritage and will advocate for constructive interaction with other nations. To further support human development, Qatar will aspire to be an active center in the fields of scientific research

and intellectual activity. The Education and Training Sector Strategy (ETSS) 2017–2022 continues the reform efforts of ETSS-1 by adding two new initiatives led by the Ministry of Education and Higher Education. The first initiative is the provision of more high-quality early childhood education opportunities; the second is ensuring that students acquire literacy and numeracy skills appropriate to their age in the first three years of school and later in years of transition from one educational stage to another.
- *Comprehensive and integrated health system.* To improve the health of Qatar's population, Qatar aspires to develop an integrated system for health care, managed according to world-class standards. This system will meet the needs of existing and future generations and provide for an increasingly healthy and lengthy life for all citizens. All health services will be accessible to the entire population. Based on the QNV 2030 pillars, the Ministry of Public Health seeks to promote public health and healthy lifestyles and provide community-based primary care as the foundation for an integrated and successful health care system. The Second National Healthcare Sector Strategy 2017–2022 (NHS-2) is based on three main pillars: better health, better care, and better value, along with a more integrated and effective health system. The NHS-2 focuses on seven priority population groups, including healthy children and adolescents, healthy women leading to healthy pregnancy and delivery, healthy and safe employees, mental health and well-being, improved health for people with multiple chronic diseases, improved health and well-being for people with special needs, and healthy aging. Furthermore, the NHS-2 emphasizes five system-wide themes: an integrated model across all levels of care for the provision of high-quality services, enhanced health promotion and disease prevention, enhanced protection from public health hazards, incorporation of the health-for-all policies approach, and an effective system of governance and leadership.
- *Labor force participation.* Qatar will strive to increase the effective labor force participation of its citizens. However, for the foreseeable future Qatar will not have enough citizens to manage the complex systems, infrastructure, and other requirements of a rapidly growing, diversifying, and technologically sophisticated economy. To realize Qatar's future ambitions, it will be necessary to make up for the shortages of local labor with expatriate workers. Attracting and retaining the right mix of skills will require appropriate incentives as well as institutional arrangements for ensuring the rights and safety of expatriate labor. The Labor Market Sector Strategy 2017–2022 focuses on rebalancing the labor market structure; increasing work efficiency in different sectors; developing the capacities of Qataris, especially highly educated women; attracting and retaining skilled and highly experienced workers; developing labor legislation; and improving the labor market information system.

SAUDI ARABIA VISION 2030

Vision 2030 is a bold yet achievable blueprint for an ambitious nation.[6] It expresses the country's long-term goals and expectations and it is built upon the country's strengths and capabilities.

The Council of Economic Affairs and Development announced 13 Vision Realization Programs (VRPs) to operationalize and guide the preparation of programs and projects toward achieving Vision 2030. At least three VRPs contribute to human capital formation:

- *The National Transformation Program (NTP)*. This program aims to achieve governmental operational excellence, improve economic enablers, and enhance living standards by accelerating the implementation of primary and digital infrastructure projects and by engaging stakeholders in identifying challenges, co-creating solutions, and contributing to the implementation of the program's initiatives. One of the primary objectives of the NTP is to transform health care by easing access to health services, improving the quality and efficiency of health care services, and promoting prevention against health risks. The second main objective is to improve living standards and safety by improving the quality of services and the urban landscape in Saudi cities, enhancing traffic safety, reducing all types of pollution, and improving the living conditions of expatriates.
- *The Quality of Life Program (QLP)*. This program aims to achieve high quality-of-life standards and develop an ecosystem to boost the participation of citizens and residents in cultural, environmental, and sports activities. According to the QLP delivery plan, the core initiatives include sports, heritage and culture, entertainment, recreation, and social engagement. Health care and education, though contributing to the QLP's final objectives, remain under the auspices of other VRPs (mostly the NTP). The QLP's ultimate ambition is to develop at least three Saudi Arabian cities into the top 100 most livable cities by 2030.
- *The Human Capabilities Development Program*. This program aims to improve the efficiency and outputs of education and training at all stages, from early education to continuing education. The program includes all components of the education and training system—such as teachers, trainers, faculty members, governance, evaluation systems, quality, curricula, educational and vocational paths—and the training environment for all stages of education.

UNITED ARAB EMIRATES VISION 2021

The United Arab Emirates Vision 2021 is guided by the National Agenda, which has four pillars relevant to human capital:[z]

- *First-rate education system*. A better education system depends on improvements in the current education system and teaching methods. Providing all schools and students with smart systems and devices is one focus. Investment in schools, including preschools, is also emphasized. Attention is given to elevating the rank of Emirati students in reading, writing, science, and the Arabic language to international standards. The pillar also aims to improve the rate of graduation from secondary schools.
- *Competitive knowledge economy*. This pillar focuses on making the transition to a knowledge-based economy, promoting innovation and research and development, strengthening the regulatory framework for key sectors, and encouraging high value–adding sectors. It strives to instill an entrepreneurial culture of leadership, creativity, responsibility, and ambition in schools and universities. It also seeks to ensure high levels of national participation in the private sector workforce.

- *World-class health care.* This pillar focuses on preventive medicine and seeks to reduce cancer and lifestyle-related diseases such as diabetes and cardiovascular diseases to ensure a longer, healthy life for citizens. It also aims to reduce the prevalence of smoking and increase the health care system's readiness to deal with epidemics and health risks.
- *Sustainable environment and infrastructure.* This pillar focuses on the government's interest in ensuring a sustainable environment and achieving a balance between economic and social development. It emphasizes the importance of air quality, preservation of water resources, clean energy, and green growth plans.

NOTES

1. *The Economic Vision 2030 for Bahrain* is available at the Bahrain government website: https://www.bahrain.bh/wps/wcm/connect/38f53f2f-9ad6-423d-9c96-2dbf17810c94/Vision%2B2030%2BEnglish%2B%28low%2Bresolution%29.pdf?MOD=AJPERES. The document was published in 2008.
2. *Kuwait Vision 2035, "New Kuwait"* is available at the Kuwait government website: http://www.newkuwait.gov.kw/home.aspx.
3. *Oman 2040* is available at the Oman government website: https://www.2040.om/en/.
4. *Qatar National Vision 2030* is available at the Qatar government website: https://www.gco.gov.qa/en/about-qatar/national-vision2030/. The document was published in 2008.
5. See the Qatar government website: https://www.psa.gov.qa/en/knowledge/Documents/NDS2Final.pdf.
6. *Vision 2030 Kingdom of Saudi Arabia* is available at the Saudi Arabia government website: https://www.vision2030.gov.sa/en.
7. *Vision 2021 United Arab Emirates* the United Arab Emirates government website: https://www.vision2021.ae/en. The document was published in 2010.

APPENDIX B

GCC Country Profiles

BAHRAIN

Bahrain

Human Capital Index Rank 47 out of 157

THE HUMAN CAPITAL INDEX (HCI) AND ITS COMPONENTS

The HCI measures the amount of human capital that a child born today can expect to attain by age 18. It conveys the productivity of the next generation of workers compared to a benchmark of complete education and full health. It is constructed for 157 countries.

It is made up of five indicators: the probability of survival to age five, a child's expected years of schooling, harmonized test scores as a measure of quality of learning, adult survival rate (fraction of 15-year olds that will survive to age 60), and the proportion of children who are not stunted.

Globally, 56 percent of all children born today will grow up to be, at best, half as productive as they could be; and 92 percent will grow up to be, at best, 75 percent as productive as they could be.

WHAT IS THE STATE OF HUMAN CAPITAL IN BAHRAIN?

- **Human Capital Index.** A child born in Bahrain today will be **67 percent** as productive when she grows up as she could be if she enjoyed complete education and full health.
- **Probability of Survival to Age 5.** 99 out of 100 children born in Bahrain survive to age 5.
- **Expected Years of School.** In Bahrain, a child who starts school at age 4 can expect to complete **13.3 years** of school by her 18th birthday.
- **Harmonized Test Scores.** Students in Bahrain score **452** on a scale where 625 represents advanced attainment and 300 represents minimum attainment.
- **Learning-adjusted Years of School.** Factoring in what children actually learn, expected years of school is only **9.6 years**.
- **Adult Survival Rate.** Across Bahrain, **93 percent** of 15-year olds will survive until age 60. This statistic is a proxy for the range of fatal and non-fatal health outcomes that a child born today would experience as an adult under current conditions.
- **Healthy Growth (Not Stunted Rate).** Data on stunting are not available for Bahrain.

ARE THERE GENDER DIFFERENCES IN HCI?

In Bahrain, the HCI for girls is higher than for boys. Table 1 shows gender disaggregation for each of the HCI components.

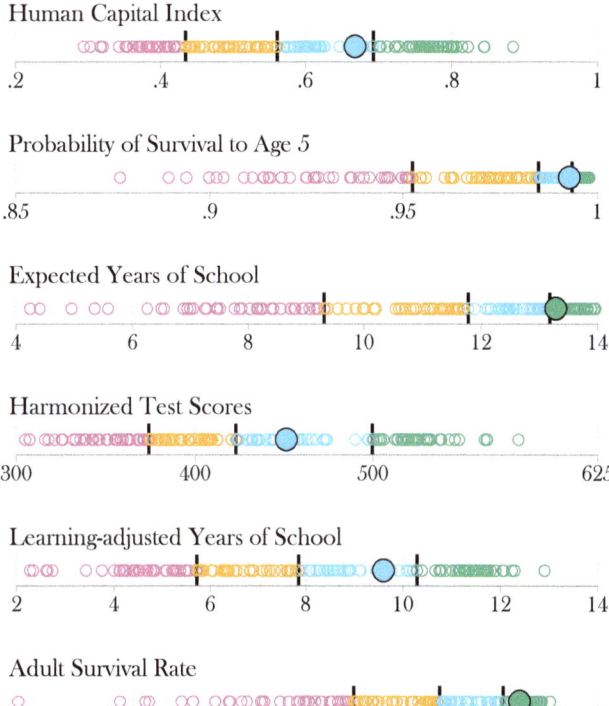

Figure 1. HCI and Components

Note:
- Large circle represents Bahrain
- Small circles represent other countries
- Thick, vertical lines and color of circles reflect quartiles of the distribution

Table 1. HCI by Gender

Component	Boys	Girls	Overall
HCI	0.64	0.7	0.67
Survival to Age 5	0.99	0.99	0.99
Expected Years of School	13.2	13.4	13.3
Harmonized Test Scores	434	470	452
Learning-adjusted Years of School	9.1	10.1	9.6
Adult Survival Rate	0.93	0.94	0.93
Not Stunted Rate	-	-	-

Note:
- When shown, hyphen denotes data are unavailable
- All values are rounded
- The gender-disaggregated HCI is calculated using only adult survival rates if gender-disaggregated stunting data is not available

#INVESTinPeople

Figure 2. Benchmarking HCI

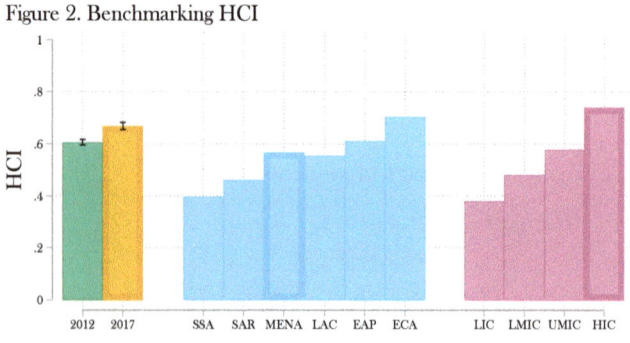

Notes:
- Unless specified all data are for 2017
- The uncertainty intervals (black vertical lines) reflect uncertainty in the measurement of components of the Index

HOW DOES BAHRAIN COMPARE?

Between 2012 and 2017, the HCI value for Bahrain increased from 0.61 to 0.67 (Figure 2).

In 2017, Bahrain's HCI is higher than the average for its region but lower than the average for its income group.

Figure 3. Learning Gap

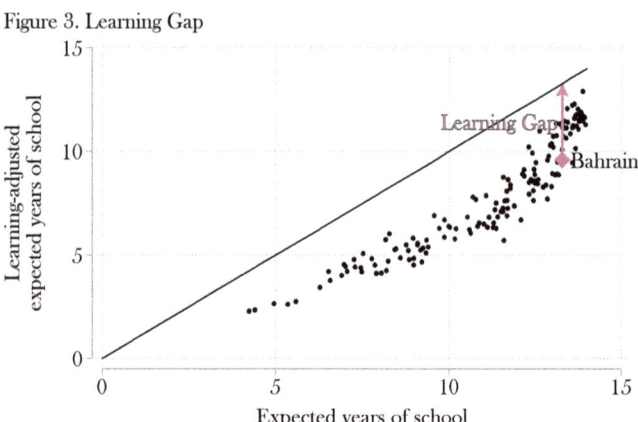

HOW MUCH ARE CHILDREN ACTUALLY LEARNING IN SCHOOL?

Children in Bahrain can expect to complete **13.3 years** of pre-primary, primary and secondary school by age 18. However, when years of schooling are adjusted for quality of learning, this is only equivalent to **9.6 years**: a learning gap of **3.7 years** (Figure 3).

Figure 4. Human Capital Index vs GDP Per Capita

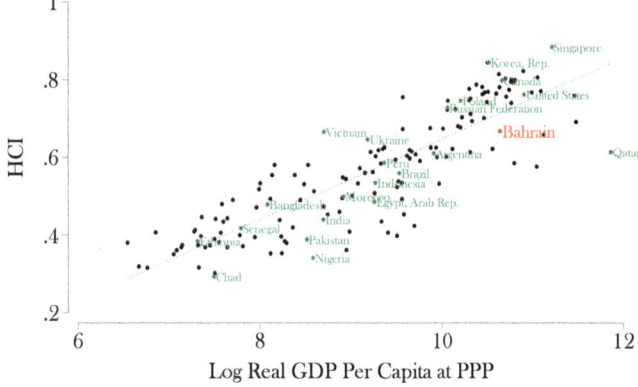

IS BAHRAIN'S HCI IN LINE WITH WHAT IS PREDICTED FOR ITS INCOME LEVEL?

In 2017, the HCI for Bahrain is lower than what would be predicted for its income level (Figure 4).

THE HUMAN CAPITAL PROJECT

The Human Capital Project seeks to raise awareness and increase demand for interventions to build human capital. It aims to accelerate better and more investments in people. The Project has three elements (i) the Human Capital Index, (ii) a program to strengthen research and measurement on human capital; and (iii) support to countries to accelerate progress in raising human capital outcomes.

For more information on the Human Capital Project please visit **www.worldbank.org/humancapitalproject**

   #investinPeople

Bahrain
Learning Poverty Brief

October 2019

AN EARLY-WARNING INDICATOR FOR THE HUMAN CAPITAL PROJECT

The Human Capital Project seeks to raise awareness and increase demand for interventions to build human capital. It aims to accelerate better and more investments in people.

In low- and middle-income countries, the learning crisis means that deficits in education outcomes are a major contributor to human capital deficits. Shortcomings in both the quantity of schooling and especially its quality explain a large part of the distance to the frontier. Addressing these shortcomings will require a multisectoral approach.

For more information on the Human Capital Project, please visit www.worldbank.org/humancapitalproject

WHY MEASURE LEARNING POVERTY?

All children should be able to read by age 10. As a major contributor to human capital deficits, the learning crisis undermines sustainable growth and poverty reduction. This brief summarizes some of the critical aspects of a new synthetic indicator, **Learning Poverty**, designed to help spotlight and galvanize action to address this crisis.

Eliminating Learning Poverty is as urgent as eliminating extreme monetary poverty, stunting, or hunger. The new data show that more than half of all children in low and middle-income countries suffer from Learning Poverty.

WHAT IS LEARNING POVERTY?

Learning Poverty means being unable to read and understand a short, age-appropriate text by age 10. All foundational skills are important, but we focus on reading because: (i) reading proficiency is an easily understood measure of learning; (ii) reading is a student's gateway to learning in every other area; and, (iii) reading proficiency can serve as a proxy for foundational learning in other subjects, in the same way that the absence of child stunting is a marker of healthy early childhood development.

HOW IS LEARNING POVERTY MEASURED?

This indicator brings together schooling and learning. It starts with the share of children who haven't achieved minimum reading proficiency and adjusts it by the proportion of children who are out of school.

$$LP = [BMP \times (1 - OoS)] + [1 \times OoS]$$

where, LP is Learning Poverty; BMP is share of children in school below minimum proficiency; OoS is the Percentage of Out-of-School children; and, in the case of OoS we assume $BMP = 1$.

The data used to calculate Learning Poverty has been made possible thanks to the work of the Global Alliance to Monitor Learning led by the UNESCO Institute for Statistics (UIS), which established Minimum Proficiency Levels (MPLs) that enable countries to benchmark learning across different cross-national and national assessments.

LEARNING POVERTY IN BAHRAIN

- **Learning Poverty.** 32 percent of children in Bahrain at late primary age today are not proficient in reading, adjusted for the Out-of-School children.
- **Out-of-School.** In Bahrain, 2 percent of primary school-aged children are not enrolled in school. These children are excluded from learning in school.
- **Below Minimum Proficiency.** Large-scale learning assessments of students in Bahrain indicate that 31 percent do not achieve the MPL at the end of primary school, proxied by data from grade 4 in 2016.

For countries with a very low Out-of-School population, the share of children Below Minimum Proficiency will be very close to the reported Learning Poverty.

Notes: The LP number for Bahrain is calculated using the Global Learning Assessment Database (GLAD) harmonization based on PIRLS and the MPL threshold used was level Low (400 points). For more details, please consult the GLAD and Learning Poverty repositories in GitHub.

BENCHMARKING BAHRAIN'S LEARNING POVERTY

Learning Poverty in Bahrain is **31.2 percentage points better than** the average for the Middle East and North Africa region and **8.2 percentage points worse than** the average for high income countries.

Figure 1. Learning Poverty and components

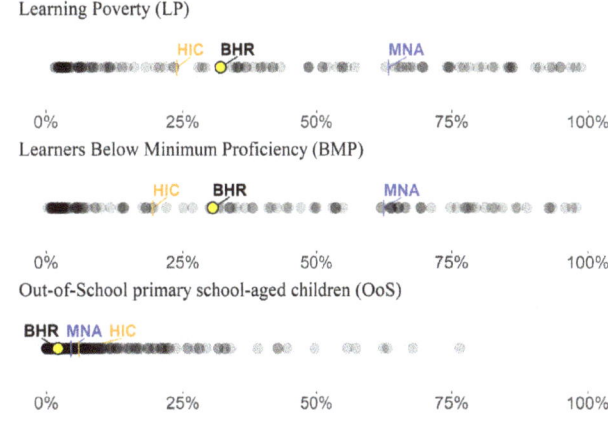

Source: UIS and World Bank as of October 2019.

Notes: (1) Large circle represents Bahrain; (2) Small circles represent other countries; and, (3) Vertical lines reflect the averages of Bahrain's region and income group.

#INVESTinPeople

Bahrain
Learning Poverty Brief

October 2019

HOW DOES BAHRAIN'S GENDER GAP COMPARE GLOBALLY?

As in most countries, **Learning Poverty is higher for boys than for girls** in Bahrain.

This result is a composition of two effects. First the share of **Out-of-School children is higher for boys** (2.9%) than for girls (1.2%).

And second **boys are less likely to achieve minimum proficiency** at the end of primary school (40.2%) than girls (21%) in Bahrain.

Table 1 shows sex disaggregation for Learning Poverty and HCI education components whenever available.

Table 1. Sex Disaggregation

Indicators and Components	Boys	Girls	All
Learning Poverty	41.9	22	32.1
Below Minimum Proficiency	40.2	21	30.6
Out-of-School	2.9	1.2	2.1
Human Capital Index	0.64	0.7	0.67
Learning-adjusted Years of Schooling	9.1	10.1	9.6

Source: UIS and World Bank for LP, BMP and OoS as of October 2019; EdStats/WDI for HCI and LAYS; The Full Learning Poverty database is available for download at the Development Data Hub.

Figure 2. Gender Gap - Learning Poverty by Sex

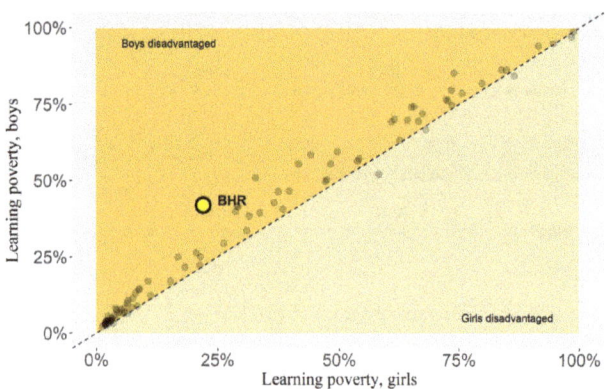

Source: UIS and World Bank as of October 2019. *Notes:* (1) - Large circle represents Bahrain; and, (2) The closer a country is to the dotted line the smaller its LP gender gap.

POINT OF CONTACT

Bahrain: Jamal Al-Kibbi

Middle East and North Africa: Laura Gregory

PRIMARY EDUCATION EXPENDITURE

Primary education expenditure per child of primary education age in Bahrain is **USD 5,350 (PPP)**, which is **3.5% below** the average for the Middle East and North Africa region and **36.4% below** the average for high income countries.

Figure 3. Expenditure per child in primary school age

Source: UIS and World Bank as of October 2019. *Note:* Primary education expenditure per child is calculated as total expenditure on primary education divided by total number of children of primary school age. Data for Bahrain is from 2015.

DATA AND DATA GAPS ON LEARNING AND SCHOOLING IN BAHRAIN

Bahrain administer a National Large-Scale Assessment (NLSA) at the End of Primary school, according to UIS SDG 4.1.2b monitoring. Once this NLSA is mapped against UIS/SDG4.1.1 reporting standards it should be possible to monitor Learning Poverty with it.

Bahrain participated in the following published cross-national learning assessments in recent years: TIMSS (2003, 2007, 2011, 2015) and PIRLS (2016).

According to the World Bank's 2013 LeAP diagnostic analysis of Bahrain's assessment system, the country's ratings on large-scale assessment activities were **Established (3 out of 4)** on Cross-National Learning Assessment and **Established (3 out of 4)** on NLSA. To update results, contact the LeAP team.

The Out-of-School adjustment in our Learning Poverty indicator relies on enrollment data. Our preferred definition is the adjusted net primary enrollment as reported by UIS. This data relies both on the population Census and the EMIS. In the case of Bahrain, the preferred definition based on the EMIS data is for 2016.

Notes: The definition of NLSA does not include National Exams; LeAP: Learning Assessment Platform (LeAP-team@worldbank.org). TIMSS: Trends in International Mathematics and Science Study. PIRLS: Progress in International Reading Literacy Study.

#investinPeople

Disclaimer: The numbers presented in this brief are based on global data harmonization efforts conducted by UIS and the World Bank that increase cross-country comparability of selected findings from official statistics. For that reason, the numbers discussed here may be different from official statistics reported by governments and national offices of statistics. Such differences are due to the different purposes of the statistics, which can be for global comparison or to meet national definitions.

#INVESTinPeople

KUWAIT

Kuwait

Human Capital Index Rank 77 out of 157

THE HUMAN CAPITAL INDEX (HCI) AND ITS COMPONENTS

The HCI measures the amount of human capital that a child born today can expect to attain by age 18. It conveys the productivity of the next generation of workers compared to a benchmark of complete education and full health. It is constructed for 157 countries.

It is made up of five indicators: the probability of survival to age five, a child's expected years of schooling, harmonized test scores as a measure of quality of learning, adult survival rate (fraction of 15-year olds that will survive to age 60), and the proportion of children who are not stunted.

Globally, 56 percent of all children born today will grow up to be, at best, half as productive as they could be; and 92 percent will grow up to be, at best, 75 percent as productive as they could be.

WHAT IS THE STATE OF HUMAN CAPITAL IN KUWAIT?

- **Human Capital Index.** A child born in Kuwait today will be **58 percent** as productive when she grows up as she could be if she enjoyed complete education and full health.

- **Probability of Survival to Age 5.** 99 out of 100 children born in Kuwait survive to age 5.

- **Expected Years of School.** In Kuwait, a child who starts school at age 4 can expect to complete **12.4 years** of school by her 18th birthday.

- **Harmonized Test Scores.** Students in Kuwait score **383** on a scale where 625 represents advanced attainment and 300 represents minimum attainment.

- **Learning-adjusted Years of School.** Factoring in what children actually learn, expected years of school is only **7.6 years**.

- **Adult Survival Rate.** Across Kuwait, **92 percent** of 15-year olds will survive until age 60. This statistic is a proxy for the range of fatal and non-fatal health outcomes that a child born today would experience as an adult under current conditions.

- **Healthy Growth (Not Stunted Rate).** 95 out of 100 children are **not** stunted. 5 out of 100 children are stunted, and so at risk of cognitive and physical limitations that can last a lifetime.

ARE THERE GENDER DIFFERENCES IN HCI?

In Kuwait, the HCI for girls is higher than for boys. Table 1 shows gender disaggregation for each of the HCI components.

Figure 1. HCI and Components

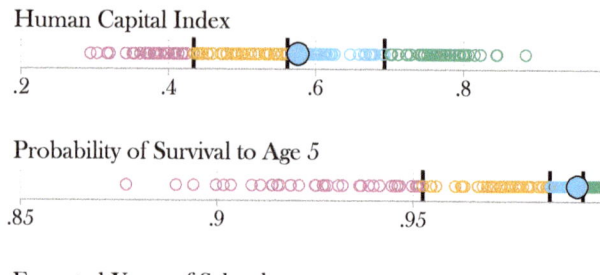

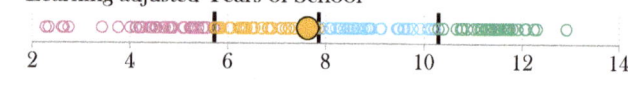

Note:
- Large circle represents Kuwait
- Small circles represent other countries
- Thick, vertical lines and color of circles reflect quartiles of the distribution

Table 1. HCI by Gender

Component	Boys	Girls	Overall
HCI	0.54	0.6	0.58
Survival to Age 5	0.99	0.99	0.99
Expected Years of School	12.1	12.8	12.4
Harmonized Test Scores	369	398	383
Learning-adjusted Years of School	7.1	8.1	7.6
Adult Survival Rate	0.91	0.94	0.92
Not Stunted Rate	-	-	0.95

Note:
- When shown, hyphen denotes data are unavailable
- All values are rounded
- The gender-disaggregated HCI is calculated using only adult survival rates if gender-disaggregated stunting data is not available

Figure 2. Benchmarking HCI

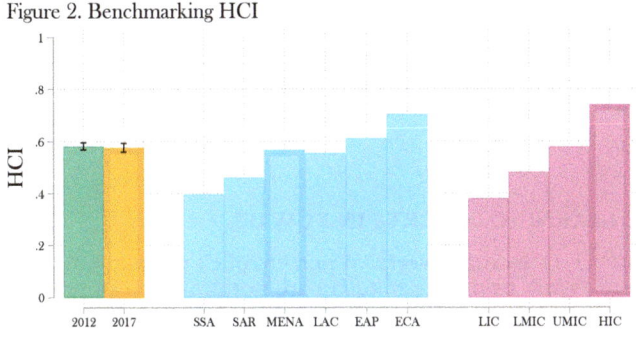

Notes:
- Unless specified all data are for 2017
- The uncertainty intervals (black vertical lines) reflect uncertainty in the measurement of components of the Index

Figure 3. Learning Gap

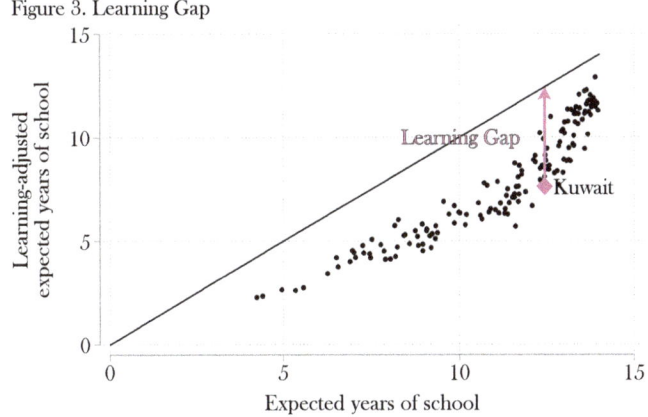

Figure 4. Human Capital Index vs GDP Per Capita

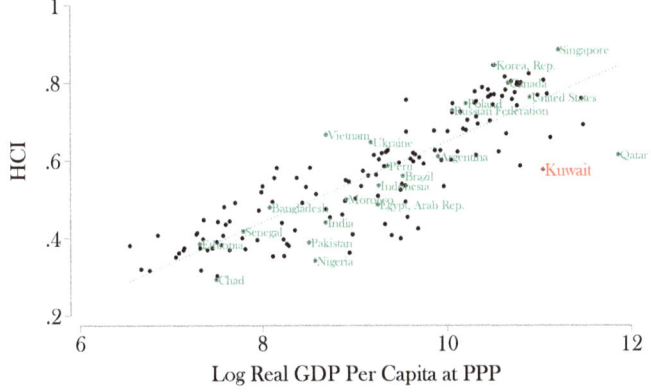

HOW DOES KUWAIT COMPARE?

Between 2012 and 2017, the HCI value for Kuwait remained approximately the same at 0.58 (Figure 2).

In 2017, Kuwait's HCI is slightly higher than the average for its region but lower than the average for its income group.

HOW MUCH ARE CHILDREN ACTUALLY LEARNING IN SCHOOL?

Children in Kuwait can expect to complete **12.4 years** of pre-primary, primary and secondary school by age 18. However, when years of schooling are adjusted for quality of learning, this is only equivalent to **7.6 years**: a learning gap of **4.8 years** (Figure 3).

IS KUWAIT'S HCI IN LINE WITH WHAT IS PREDICTED FOR ITS INCOME LEVEL?

In 2017, the HCI for Kuwait is lower than what would be predicted for its income level (Figure 4).

THE HUMAN CAPITAL PROJECT

The Human Capital Project seeks to raise awareness and increase demand for interventions to build human capital. It aims to accelerate better and more investments in people. The Project has three elements (i) the Human Capital Index, (ii) a program to strengthen research and measurement on human capital; and (iii) support to countries to accelerate progress in raising human capital outcomes.

For more information on the Human Capital Project please visit **www.worldbank.org/humancapitalproject**

 #investinPeople

Kuwait
Learning Poverty Brief

October 2019

AN EARLY-WARNING INDICATOR FOR THE HUMAN CAPITAL PROJECT

The Human Capital Project seeks to raise awareness and increase demand for interventions to build human capital. It aims to accelerate better and more investments in people.

In low- and middle-income countries, the learning crisis means that deficits in education outcomes are a major contributor to human capital deficits. Shortcomings in both the quantity of schooling and especially its quality explain a large part of the distance to the frontier. Addressing these shortcomings will require a multisectoral approach.

For more information on the Human Capital Project, please visit www.worldbank.org/humancapitalproject

WHY MEASURE LEARNING POVERTY?

All children should be able to read by age 10. As a major contributor to human capital deficits, the learning crisis undermines sustainable growth and poverty reduction. This brief summarizes some of the critical aspects of a new synthetic indicator, **Learning Poverty**, designed to help spotlight and galvanize action to address this crisis.

Eliminating Learning Poverty is as urgent as eliminating extreme monetary poverty, stunting, or hunger. The new data show that more than half of all children in low and middle-income countries suffer from Learning Poverty.

WHAT IS LEARNING POVERTY?

Learning Poverty means being unable to read and understand a short, age-appropriate text by age 10. All foundational skills are important, but we focus on reading because: (i) reading proficiency is an easily understood measure of learning; (ii) reading is a student's gateway to learning in every other area; and, (iii) reading proficiency can serve as a proxy for foundational learning in other subjects, in the same way that the absence of child stunting is a marker of healthy early childhood development.

HOW IS LEARNING POVERTY MEASURED?

This indicator brings together schooling and learning. It starts with the share of children who haven't achieved minimum reading proficiency and adjusts it by the proportion of children who are out of school.

$$LP = [BMP \times (1 - OoS)] + [1 \times OoS]$$

where, LP is Learning Poverty; BMP is share of children in school below minimum proficiency; OoS is the Percentage of Out-of-School children; and, in the case of OoS we assume $BMP = 1$.

The data used to calculate Learning Poverty has been made possible thanks to the work of the Global Alliance to Monitor Learning led by the UNESCO Institute for Statistics (UIS), which established Minimum Proficiency Levels (MPLs) that enable countries to benchmark learning across different cross-national and national assessments.

LEARNING POVERTY IN KUWAIT

- **Learning Poverty.** 51 percent of children in Kuwait at late primary age today are not proficient in reading, adjusted for the Out-of-School children.
- **Out-of-School.** In Kuwait, 3 percent of primary school-aged children are not enrolled in school. These children are excluded from learning in school.
- **Below Minimum Proficiency.** Large-scale learning assessments of students in Kuwait indicate that 49 percent do not achieve the MPL at the end of primary school, proxied by data from grade 4 in 2016.

For countries with a very low Out-of-School population, the share of children Below Minimum Proficiency will be very close to the reported Learning Poverty.

Notes: The LP number for Kuwait is calculated using the Global Learning Assessment Database (GLAD) harmonization based on PIRLS and the MPL threshold used was level Low (400 points). For more details, please consult the GLAD and Learning Poverty repositories in GitHub.

BENCHMARKING KUWAIT'S LEARNING POVERTY

Learning Poverty in Kuwait is **12.3 percentage points better than** the average for the Middle East and North Africa region and **27.1 percentage points worse than** the average for high income countries.

Figure 1. Learning Poverty and components

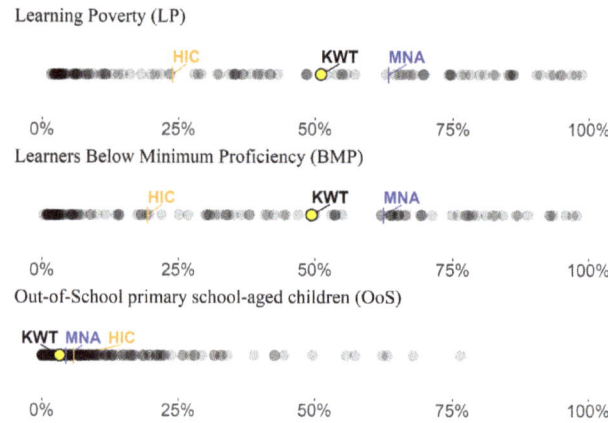

Source: UIS and World Bank as of October 2019.
Notes: (1) Large circle represents Kuwait; (2) Small circles represent other countries; and, (3) Vertical lines reflect the averages of Kuwait's region and income group.

#INVESTinPeople

Kuwait
Learning Poverty Brief

October 2019

HOW DOES KUWAIT'S GENDER GAP COMPARE GLOBALLY?

As in most countries, **Learning Poverty is higher for boys than for girls** in Kuwait.

This result is a composition of two effects. First the share of **Out-of-School children is higher for boys** (5%) than for girls (1.4%).

And second **boys are less likely to achieve minimum proficiency** at the end of primary school (56%) than girls (43.3%) in Kuwait.

Table 1 shows sex disaggregation for Learning Poverty and HCI education components whenever available.

Table 1. Sex Disaggregation

Indicators and Components	Boys	Girls	All
Learning Poverty	58.2	44.1	51
Below Minimum Proficiency	56	43.3	49.4
Out-of-School	5	1.4	3.3
Human Capital Index	0.54	0.6	0.58
Learning-adjusted Years of Schooling	7.1	8.1	7.6

Source: UIS and World Bank for LP, BMP and OoS as of October 2019; EdStats/WDI for HCI and LAYS; The Full Learning Poverty database is available for download at the Development Data Hub.

Figure 2. Gender Gap - Learning Poverty by Sex

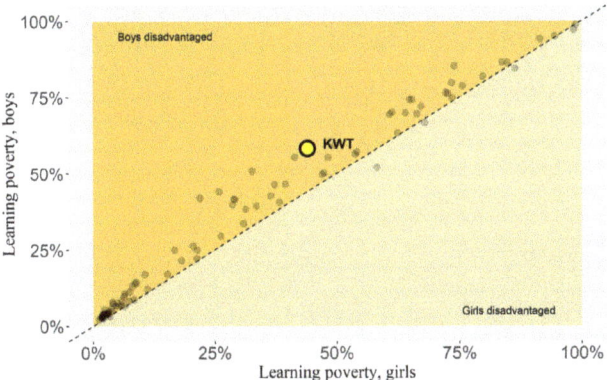

Source: UIS and World Bank as of October 2019. *Notes:* (1) - Large circle represents Kuwait; and, (2) The closer a country is to the dotted line the smaller its LP gender gap.

POINT OF CONTACT
Kuwait: Laura Gregory and Hiba Ahmed
Middle East and North Africa: Laura Gregory

PRIMARY EDUCATION EXPENDITURE

Primary education expenditure per child of primary education age in Kuwait is **USD 11,966 (PPP)**, which is **115.7% above** the average for the Middle East and North Africa region and **42.3% above** the average for high income countries.

Figure 3. Expenditure per child in primary school age

Source: UIS and World Bank as of October 2019. *Note:* Primary education expenditure per child is calculated as total expenditure on primary education divided by total number of children of primary school age. Data for Kuwait is from 2014.

DATA AND DATA GAPS ON LEARNING AND SCHOOLING IN KUWAIT

Kuwait does not administer a National Large-Scale Assessment (NLSA) at the End of Primary school, according to UIS SDG 4.1.2b monitoring.

Kuwait participated in the following published cross-national learning assessments in recent years: TIMSS (2007, 2011, 2015) and PIRLS (2001, 2011, 2016, 2006).

According to the World Bank's 2011 LeAP diagnostic analysis of Kuwait's assessment system, the country's ratings on large-scale assessment activities were **Emerging (2 out of 4)** on Cross-National Learning Assessment and **Latent (1 out of 4)** on NLSA. To update results, contact the LeAP team.

The Out-of-School adjustment in our Learning Poverty indicator relies on enrollment data. Our preferred definition is the adjusted net primary enrollment as reported by UIS. This data relies both on the population Census and the EMIS. In the case of Kuwait, the preferred definition based on the EMIS data is for 2016.

Notes: The definition of NLSA does not include National Exams; LeAP: Learning Assessment Platform (LeAP-team@worldbank.org). TIMSS: Trends in International Mathematics and Science Study. PIRLS: Progress in International Reading Literacy Study.

#investinPeople

Disclaimer: The numbers presented in this brief are based on global data harmonization efforts conducted by UIS and the World Bank that increase cross-country comparability of selected findings from official statistics. For that reason, the numbers discussed here may be different from official statistics reported by governments and national offices of statistics. Such differences are due to the different purposes of the statistics, which can be for global comparison or to meet national definitions.

OMAN

Oman

Human Capital Index Rank 54 out of 157

THE HUMAN CAPITAL INDEX (HCI) AND ITS COMPONENTS

The HCI measures the amount of human capital that a child born today can expect to attain by age 18. It conveys the productivity of the next generation of workers compared to a benchmark of complete education and full health. It is constructed for 157 countries.

It is made up of five indicators: the probability of survival to age five, a child's expected years of schooling, harmonized test scores as a measure of quality of learning, adult survival rate (fraction of 15-year olds that will survive to age 60), and the proportion of children who are not stunted.

Globally, 56 percent of all children born today will grow up to be, at best, half as productive as they could be; and 92 percent will grow up to be, at best, 75 percent as productive as they could be.

WHAT IS THE STATE OF HUMAN CAPITAL IN OMAN?

- **Human Capital Index.** A child born in Oman today will be **62 percent** as productive when she grows up as she could be if she enjoyed complete education and full health.
- **Probability of Survival to Age 5.** 99 out of 100 children born in Oman survive to age 5.
- **Expected Years of School.** In Oman, a child who starts school at age 4 can expect to complete **13.1 years** of school by her 18th birthday.
- **Harmonized Test Scores.** Students in Oman score **424** on a scale where 625 represents advanced attainment and 300 represents minimum attainment.
- **Learning-adjusted Years of School.** Factoring in what children actually learn, expected years of school is only **8.9 years**.
- **Adult Survival Rate.** Across Oman, **91 percent** of 15-year olds will survive until age 60. This statistic is a proxy for the range of fatal and non-fatal health outcomes that a child born today would experience as an adult under current conditions.
- **Healthy Growth (Not Stunted Rate).** 86 out of 100 children are **not** stunted. 14 out of 100 children are stunted, and so at risk of cognitive and physical limitations that can last a lifetime.

ARE THERE GENDER DIFFERENCES IN HCI?

In Oman, the HCI for girls is higher than for boys. Table 1 shows gender disaggregation for each of the HCI components.

Figure 1. HCI and Components

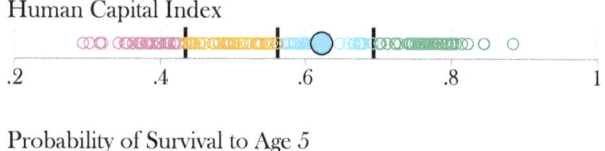

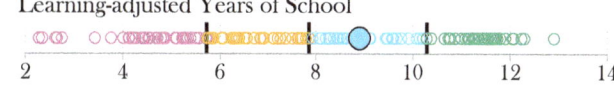

Note:
- Large circle represents Oman
- Small circles represent other countries
- Thick, vertical lines and color of circles reflect quartiles of the distribution

Table 1. HCI by Gender

Component	Boys	Girls	Overall
HCI	0.59	0.66	0.62
Survival to Age 5	0.99	0.99	0.99
Expected Years of School	13	13.3	13.1
Harmonized Test Scores	404	444	424
Learning-adjusted Years of School	8.4	9.4	8.9
Adult Survival Rate	0.9	0.93	0.91
Not Stunted Rate	-	-	0.86

Note:
- When shown, hyphen denotes data are unavailable
- All values are rounded
- The gender-disaggregated HCI is calculated using only adult survival rates if gender-disaggregated stunting data is not available

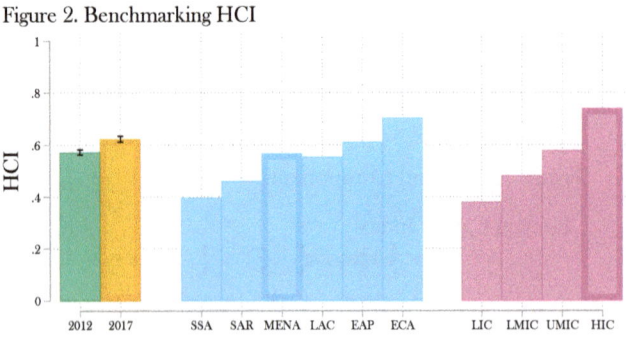

Figure 2. Benchmarking HCI

Notes:
- Unless specified all data are for 2017
- The uncertainty intervals (black vertical lines) reflect uncertainty in the measurement of components of the Index

HOW DOES OMAN COMPARE?

Between 2012 and 2017, the HCI value for Oman increased from 0.57 to 0.62 (Figure 2).

In 2017, Oman's HCI is higher than the average for its region but lower than the average for its income group.

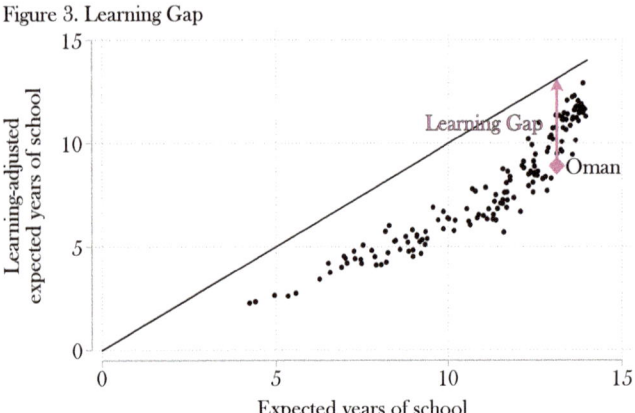

Figure 3. Learning Gap

HOW MUCH ARE CHILDREN ACTUALLY LEARNING IN SCHOOL?

Children in Oman can expect to complete **13.1 years** of pre-primary, primary and secondary school by age 18. However, when years of schooling are adjusted for quality of learning, this is only equivalent to **8.9 years**: a learning gap of **4.2 years** (Figure 3).

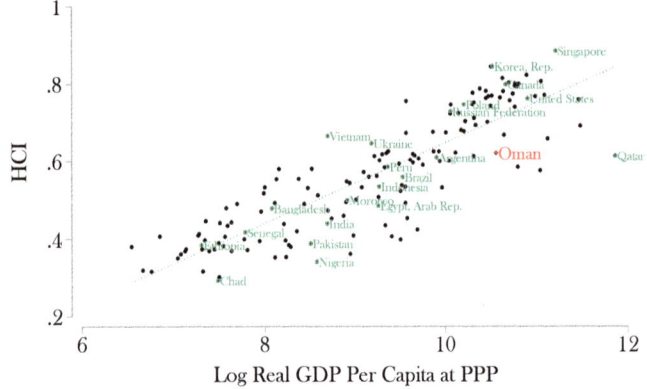

Figure 4. Human Capital Index vs GDP Per Capita

IS OMAN'S HCI IN LINE WITH WHAT IS PREDICTED FOR ITS INCOME LEVEL?

In 2017, the HCI for Oman is lower than what would be predicted for its income level (Figure 4).

THE HUMAN CAPITAL PROJECT

The Human Capital Project seeks to raise awareness and increase demand for interventions to build human capital. It aims to accelerate better and more investments in people. The Project has three elements (i) the Human Capital Index, (ii) a program to strengthen research and measurement on human capital; and (iii) support to countries to accelerate progress in raising human capital outcomes.

For more information on the Human Capital Project please visit **www.worldbank.org/humancapitalproject**

 #investinPeople

Oman
Learning Poverty Brief

October 2019

AN EARLY-WARNING INDICATOR FOR THE HUMAN CAPITAL PROJECT

The Human Capital Project seeks to raise awareness and increase demand for interventions to build human capital. It aims to accelerate better and more investments in people.

In low- and middle-income countries, the learning crisis means that deficits in education outcomes are a major contributor to human capital deficits. Shortcomings in both the quantity of schooling and especially its quality explain a large part of the distance to the frontier. Addressing these shortcomings will require a multisectoral approach.

For more information on the Human Capital Project, please visit **www.worldbank.org/humancapitalproject**

WHY MEASURE LEARNING POVERTY?

All children should be able to read by age 10. As a major contributor to human capital deficits, the learning crisis undermines sustainable growth and poverty reduction. This brief summarizes some of the critical aspects of a new synthetic indicator, **Learning Poverty**, designed to help spotlight and galvanize action to address this crisis.

Eliminating Learning Poverty is as urgent as eliminating extreme monetary poverty, stunting, or hunger. The new data show that more than half of all children in low and middle-income countries suffer from Learning Poverty.

WHAT IS LEARNING POVERTY?

Learning Poverty means being unable to read and understand a short, age-appropriate text by age 10. All foundational skills are important, but we focus on reading because: (i) reading proficiency is an easily understood measure of learning; (ii) reading is a student's gateway to learning in every other area; and, (iii) reading proficiency can serve as a proxy for foundational learning in other subjects, in the same way that the absence of child stunting is a marker of healthy early childhood development.

HOW IS LEARNING POVERTY MEASURED?

This indicator brings together schooling and learning. It starts with the share of children who haven't achieved minimum reading proficiency and adjusts it by the proportion of children who are out of school.

$$LP = [BMP \times (1 - OoS)] + [1 \times OoS]$$

where, LP is Learning Poverty; BMP is share of children in school below minimum proficiency; OoS is the Percentage of Out-of-School children; and, in the case of OoS we assume $BMP = 1$.

The data used to calculate Learning Poverty has been made possible thanks to the work of the Global Alliance to Monitor Learning led by the UNESCO Institute for Statistics (UIS), which established Minimum Proficiency Levels (MPLs) that enable countries to benchmark learning across different cross-national and national assessments.

LEARNING POVERTY IN OMAN

- **Learning Poverty.** 42 percent of children in Oman at late primary age today are not proficient in reading, adjusted for the Out-of-School children.
- **Out-of-School.** In Oman, 1 percent of primary school-aged children are not enrolled in school. These children are excluded from learning in school.
- **Below Minimum Proficiency.** Large-scale learning assessments of students in Oman indicate that 41 percent do not achieve the MPL at the end of primary school, proxied by data from grade 4 in 2016.

For countries with a very low Out-of-School population, the share of children Below Minimum Proficiency will be very close to the reported Learning Poverty.

Notes: The LP number for Oman is calculated using the Global Learning Assessment Database (GLAD) harmonization based on PIRLS and the MPL threshold used was level Low (400 points). For more details, please consult the GLAD and Learning Poverty repositories in GitHub.

BENCHMARKING OMAN'S LEARNING POVERTY

Learning Poverty in Oman is **21.5 percentage points better than** the average for the Middle East and North Africa region and **17.9 percentage points worse than** the average for high income countries.

Figure 1. Learning Poverty and components

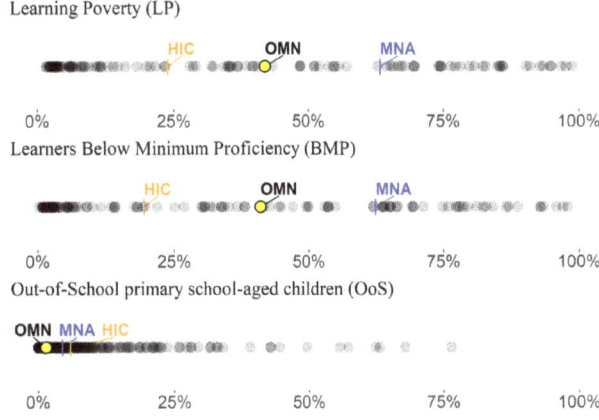

Source: UIS and World Bank as of October 2019.
Notes: (1) Large circle represents Oman; (2) Small circles represent other countries; and, (3) Vertical lines reflect the averages of Oman's region and income group.

#INVESTinPeople

Oman
Learning Poverty Brief

October 2019

HOW DOES OMAN'S GENDER GAP COMPARE GLOBALLY?

As in most countries, **Learning Poverty is higher for boys than for girls** in Oman.

This result is a composition of two effects. First the share of **Out-of-School children is higher for boys** (1.5%) than for girls (1.4%).

And second **boys are less likely to achieve minimum proficiency** at the end of primary school (50%) than girls (31.9%) in Oman.

Table 1 shows sex disaggregation for Learning Poverty and HCI education components whenever available.

Table 1. Sex Disaggregation

Indicators and Components	Boys	Girls	All
Learning Poverty	50.8	32.8	41.8
Below Minimum Proficiency	50	31.9	40.9
Out-of-School	1.5	1.4	1.5
Human Capital Index	0.59	0.66	0.62
Learning-adjusted Years of Schooling	8.4	9.4	8.9

Source: UIS and World Bank for LP, BMP and OoS as of October 2019; EdStats/WDI for HCI and LAYS; The Full Learning Poverty database is available for download at the Development Data Hub.

Figure 2. Gender Gap - Learning Poverty by Sex

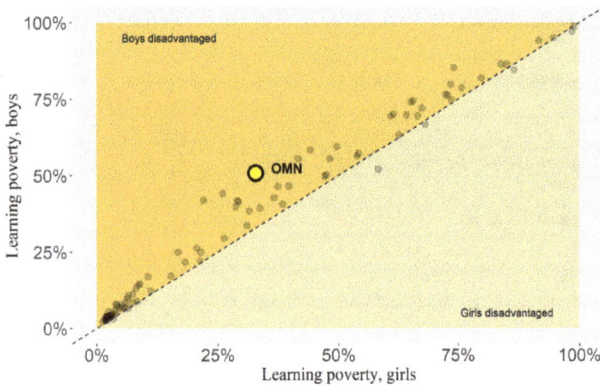

Source: UIS and World Bank as of October 2019. *Notes:* (1) - Large circle represents Oman; and, (2) The closer a country is to the dotted line the smaller its LP gender gap.

POINT OF CONTACT

Oman: Igor Kheyftes

Middle East and North Africa: Laura Gregory

PRIMARY EDUCATION EXPENDITURE

Primary education expenditure per child of primary education age in Oman is **USD 13,422 (PPP)**, which is **142% above** the average for the Middle East and North Africa region and **59.6% above** the average for high income countries.

Figure 3. Expenditure per child in primary school age

Source: UIS and World Bank as of October 2019. *Note:* Primary education expenditure per child is calculated as total expenditure on primary education divided by total number of children of primary school age. Data for Oman is from 2017.

DATA AND DATA GAPS ON LEARNING AND SCHOOLING IN OMAN

Oman administer a National Large-Scale Assessment (NLSA) at the End of Primary school, according to UIS SDG 4.1.2b monitoring. Once this NLSA is mapped against UIS/SDG4.1.1 reporting standards it should be possible to monitor Learning Poverty with it.

Oman participated in the following published cross-national learning assessments in recent years: TIMSS (2007, 2011, 2015) and PIRLS (2011, 2016).

According to the World Bank's 2013 LeAP diagnostic analysis of Oman's assessment system, the country's ratings on large-scale assessment activities were **Established (3 out of 4)** on Cross-National Learning Assessment and **Established (3 out of 4)** on NLSA. To update results, contact the LeAP team.

The Out-of-School adjustment in our Learning Poverty indicator relies on enrollment data. Our preferred definition is the adjusted net primary enrollment as reported by UIS. This data relies both on the population Census and the EMIS. In the case of Oman, the preferred definition based on the EMIS data is for 2016.

Notes: The definition of NLSA does not include National Exams; LeAP: Learning Assessment Platform (LeAP-team@worldbank.org). TIMSS: Trends in International Mathematics and Science Study. PIRLS: Progress in International Reading Literacy Study.

 #investinPeople

Disclaimer: The numbers presented in this brief are based on global data harmonization efforts conducted by UIS and the World Bank that increase cross-country comparability of selected findings from official statistics. For that reason, the numbers discussed here may be different from official statistics reported by governments and national offices of statistics. Such differences are due to the different purposes of the statistics, which can be for global comparison or to meet national definitions.

#INVESTinPeople

QATAR

Qatar

Human Capital Index Rank 60 out of 157

THE HUMAN CAPITAL INDEX (HCI) AND ITS COMPONENTS

The HCI measures the amount of human capital that a child born today can expect to attain by age 18. It conveys the productivity of the next generation of workers compared to a benchmark of complete education and full health. It is constructed for 157 countries.

It is made up of five indicators: the probability of survival to age five, a child's expected years of schooling, harmonized test scores as a measure of quality of learning, adult survival rate (fraction of 15-year olds that will survive to age 60), and the proportion of children who are not stunted.

Globally, 56 percent of all children born today will grow up to be, at best, half as productive as they could be; and 92 percent will grow up to be, at best, 75 percent as productive as they could be.

WHAT IS THE STATE OF HUMAN CAPITAL IN QATAR?

- **Human Capital Index.** A child born in Qatar today will be **61 percent** as productive when she grows up as she could be if she enjoyed complete education and full health.

- **Probability of Survival to Age 5.** **99** out of 100 children born in Qatar survive to age 5.

- **Expected Years of School.** In Qatar, a child who starts school at age 4 can expect to complete **12.3 years** of school by her 18th birthday.

- **Harmonized Test Scores.** Students in Qatar score **432** on a scale where 625 represents advanced attainment and 300 represents minimum attainment.

- **Learning-adjusted Years of School.** Factoring in what children actually learn, expected years of school is only **8.5 years**.

- **Adult Survival Rate.** Across Qatar, **94 percent** of 15-year olds will survive until age 60. This statistic is a proxy for the range of fatal and non-fatal health outcomes that a child born today would experience as an adult under current conditions.

- **Healthy Growth (Not Stunted Rate).** Data on stunting are not available for Qatar.

ARE THERE GENDER DIFFERENCES IN HCI?

In Qatar, the HCI for girls is higher than for boys. Table 1 shows gender disaggregation for each of the HCI components.

Figure 1. HCI and Components

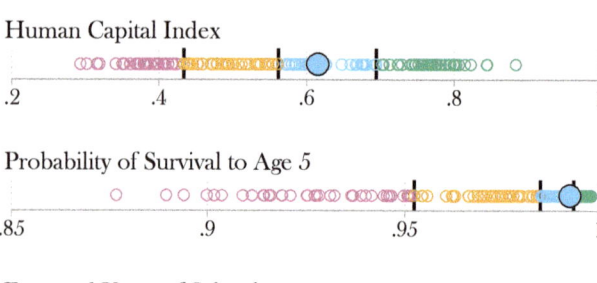

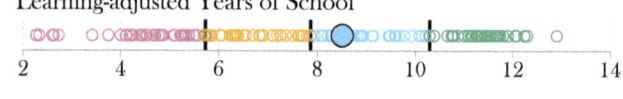

Note:
- Large circle represents Qatar
- Small circles represent other countries
- Thick, vertical lines and color of circles reflect quartiles of the distribution

Table 1. HCI by Gender

Component	Boys	Girls	Overall
HCI	0.59	0.65	0.61
Survival to Age 5	0.99	0.99	0.99
Expected Years of School	11.9	12.8	12.3
Harmonized Test Scores	418	446	432
Learning-adjusted Years of School	8	9.2	8.5
Adult Survival Rate	0.94	0.95	0.94
Not Stunted Rate	-	-	-

Note:
- When shown, hyphen denotes data are unavailable
- All values are rounded
- The gender-disaggregated HCI is calculated using only adult survival rates if gender-disaggregated stunting data is not available

Figure 2. Benchmarking HCI

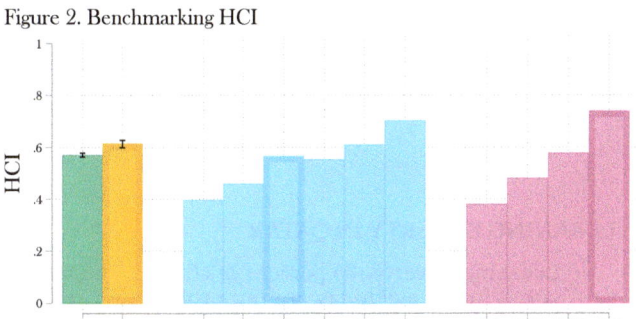

Notes:
- Unless specified all data are for 2017
- The uncertainty intervals (black vertical lines) reflect uncertainty in the measurement of components of the Index

HOW DOES QATAR COMPARE?

Between 2012 and 2017, the HCI value for Qatar increased from 0.57 to 0.61 (Figure 2).

In 2017, Qatar's HCI is higher than the average for its region but lower than the average for its income group.

Figure 3. Learning Gap

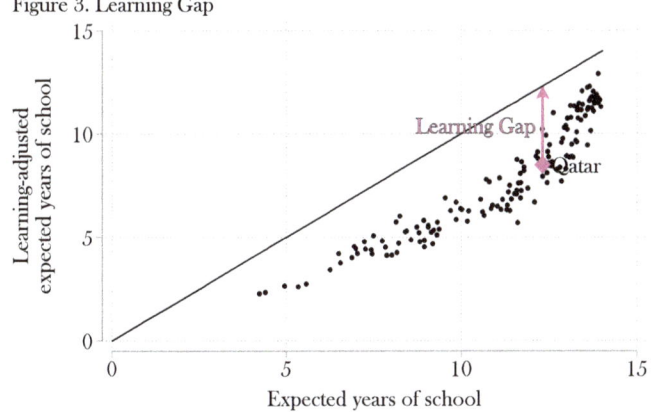

HOW MUCH ARE CHILDREN ACTUALLY LEARNING IN SCHOOL?

Children in Qatar can expect to complete **12.3 years** of pre-primary, primary and secondary school by age 18. However, when years of schooling are adjusted for quality of learning, this is only equivalent to **8.5 years**: a learning gap of **3.8 years** (Figure 3).

Figure 4. Human Capital Index vs GDP Per Capita

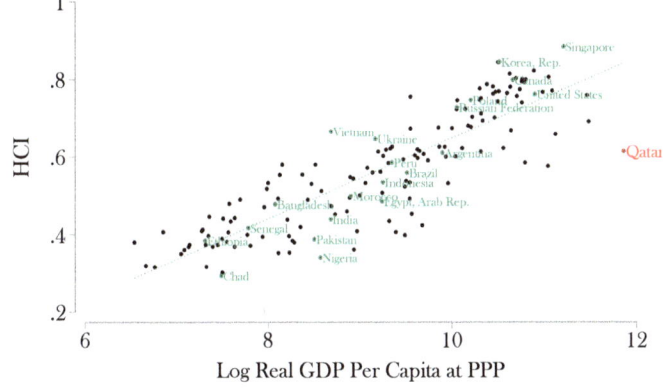

IS QATAR'S HCI IN LINE WITH WHAT IS PREDICTED FOR ITS INCOME LEVEL?

In 2017, the HCI for Qatar is lower than what would be predicted for its income level (Figure 4).

THE HUMAN CAPITAL PROJECT

The Human Capital Project seeks to raise awareness and increase demand for interventions to build human capital. It aims to accelerate better and more investments in people. The Project has three elements (i) the Human Capital Index, (ii) a program to strengthen research and measurement on human capital; and (iii) support to countries to accelerate progress in raising human capital outcomes.

For more information on the Human Capital Project please visit **www.worldbank.org/humancapitalproject**

 #**invest**inPeople

Qatar
Learning Poverty Brief

October 2019

AN EARLY-WARNING INDICATOR FOR THE HUMAN CAPITAL PROJECT

The Human Capital Project seeks to raise awareness and increase demand for interventions to build human capital. It aims to accelerate better and more investments in people.

In low- and middle-income countries, the learning crisis means that deficits in education outcomes are a major contributor to human capital deficits. Shortcomings in both the quantity of schooling and especially its quality explain a large part of the distance to the frontier. Addressing these shortcomings will require a multisectoral approach.

For more information on the Human Capital Project, please visit **www.worldbank.org/humancapitalproject**

WHY MEASURE LEARNING POVERTY?

All children should be able to read by age 10. As a major contributor to human capital deficits, the learning crisis undermines sustainable growth and poverty reduction. This brief summarizes some of the critical aspects of a new synthetic indicator, **Learning Poverty**, designed to help spotlight and galvanize action to address this crisis.

Eliminating Learning Poverty is as urgent as eliminating extreme monetary poverty, stunting, or hunger. The new data show that more than half of all children in low and middle-income countries suffer from Learning Poverty.

WHAT IS LEARNING POVERTY?

Learning Poverty means being unable to read and understand a short, age-appropriate text by age 10. All foundational skills are important, but we focus on reading because: (i) reading proficiency is an easily understood measure of learning; (ii) reading is a student's gateway to learning in every other area; and, (iii) reading proficiency can serve as a proxy for foundational learning in other subjects, in the same way that the absence of child stunting is a marker of healthy early childhood development.

HOW IS LEARNING POVERTY MEASURED?

This indicator brings together schooling and learning. It starts with the share of children who haven't achieved minimum reading proficiency and adjusts it by the proportion of children who are out of school.

$$LP = [BMP \times (1 - OoS)] + [1 \times OoS]$$

where, LP is Learning Poverty; BMP is share of children in school below minimum proficiency; OoS is the Percentage of Out-of-School children; and, in the case of OoS we assume $BMP = 1$.

The data used to calculate Learning Poverty has been made possible thanks to the work of the Global Alliance to Monitor Learning led by the UNESCO Institute for Statistics (UIS), which established Minimum Proficiency Levels (MPLs) that enable countries to benchmark learning across different cross-national and national assessments.

LEARNING POVERTY IN QATAR

- **Learning Poverty.** 35 percent of children in Qatar at late primary age today are not proficient in reading, adjusted for the Out-of-School children.
- **Out-of-School.** In Qatar, 2 percent of primary school-aged children are not enrolled in school. These children are excluded from learning in school.
- **Below Minimum Proficiency.** Large-scale learning assessments of students in Qatar indicate that 34 percent do not achieve the MPL at the end of primary school, proxied by data from grade 4 in 2016.

For countries with a very low Out-of-School population, the share of children Below Minimum Proficiency will be very close to the reported Learning Poverty.

Notes: The LP number for Qatar is calculated using the Global Learning Assessment Database (GLAD) harmonization based on PIRLS and the MPL threshold used was level Low (400 points). For more details, please consult the GLAD and Learning Poverty repositories in GitHub.

BENCHMARKING QATAR'S LEARNING POVERTY

Learning Poverty in Qatar is **28 percentage points better than** the average for the Middle East and North Africa region and **11.4 percentage points worse than** the average for high income countries.

Figure 1. Learning Poverty and components

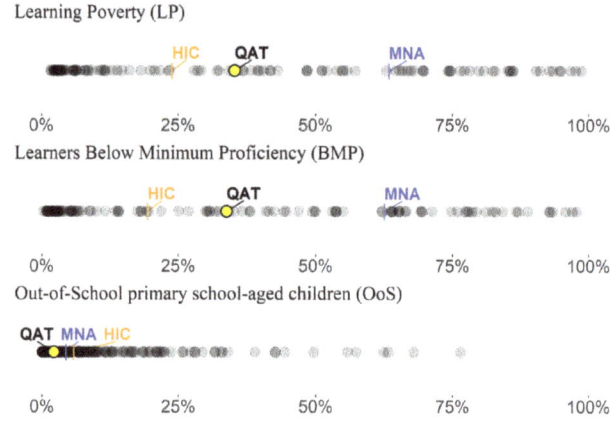

Source: UIS and World Bank as of October 2019.

Notes: (1) Large circle represents Qatar; (2) Small circles represent other countries; and, (3) Vertical lines reflect the averages of Qatar's region and income group.

#INVESTinPeople

Qatar
Learning Poverty Brief

October 2019

HOW DOES QATAR'S GENDER GAP COMPARE GLOBALLY?

As in most countries, **Learning Poverty is higher for boys than for girls** in Qatar.

This result is a composition of two effects. First the share of **Out-of-School children is lower for boys** (2%) than for girls (2.4%).

And second **boys are less likely to achieve minimum proficiency** at the end of primary school (40.4%) than girls (27.3%) in Qatar.

Table 1 shows sex disaggregation for Learning Poverty and HCI education components whenever available.

Table 1. Sex Disaggregation

Indicators and Components	Boys	Girls	All
Learning Poverty	41.6	29	35.3
Below Minimum Proficiency	40.4	27.3	33.8
Out-of-School	2	2.4	2.2
Human Capital Index	0.59	0.65	0.62
Learning-adjusted Years of Schooling	7.9	9.1	8.5

Source: UIS and World Bank for LP, BMP and OoS as of October 2019; EdStats/WDI for HCI and LAYS; The Full Learning Poverty database is available for download at the Development Data Hub.

Figure 2. Gender Gap - Learning Poverty by Sex

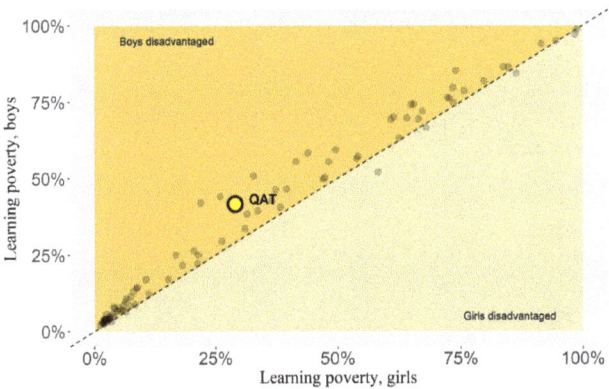

Source: UIS and World Bank as of October 2019. *Notes:* (1) - Large circle represents Qatar; and, (2) The closer a country is to the dotted line the smaller its LP gender gap.

POINT OF CONTACT

Qatar: Simon Thacker

Middle East and North Africa: Laura Gregory

PRIMARY EDUCATION EXPENDITURE

Primary education expenditure per child of primary education age in Qatar is **USD 13,541 (PPP)**, which is **144.1% above** the average for the Middle East and North Africa region and **61% above** the average for high income countries.

Figure 3. Expenditure per child in primary school age

Source: UIS and World Bank as of October 2019. *Note:* Primary education expenditure per child is calculated as total expenditure on primary education divided by total number of children of primary school age. Data for Qatar is from 2009.

DATA AND DATA GAPS ON LEARNING AND SCHOOLING IN QATAR

Qatar administer a National Large-Scale Assessment (NLSA) at the End of Primary school, according to UIS SDG 4.1.2b monitoring. Once this NLSA is mapped against UIS/SDG4.1.1 reporting standards it should be possible to monitor Learning Poverty with it.

Qatar participated in the following published cross-national learning assessments in recent years: TIMSS (2007, 2011, 2015), PIRLS (2011, 2016, 2006) and PISA (2006, 2009, 2012, 2015).

Qatar has not participated in the World Bank's LeAP diagnostic exercise to analyze its assessment system. To get started, contact the LeAP team.

The Out-of-School adjustment in our Learning Poverty indicator relies on enrollment data. Our preferred definition is the adjusted net primary enrollment as reported by UIS. This data relies both on the population Census and the EMIS. In the case of Qatar, the preferred definition based on the EMIS data is for 2016.

Notes: The definition of NLSA does not include National Exams; LeAP: Learning Assessment Platform (LeAP-team@worldbank.org). TIMSS: Trends in International Mathematics and Science Study. PIRLS: Progress in International Reading Literacy Study. PISA: Programme for International Student Assessment.

 #investinPeople

Disclaimer: The numbers presented in this brief are based on global data harmonization efforts conducted by UIS and the World Bank that increase cross-country comparability of selected findings from official statistics. For that reason, the numbers discussed here may be different from official statistics reported by governments and national offices of statistics. Such differences are due to the different purposes of the statistics, which can be for global comparison or to meet national definitions.

#INVESTinPeople

Middle East & North Africa

QATAR
PISA 2018

TAKEAWAYS

Qatar is one of the only seven countries in PISA 2018 showing a continued improvement in all three subjects, but gender and socioeconomic status-related performance gaps keep widening.

- Scores in every subject have moved close to or above the MENA average. Yet, student performance is roughly 2.5 years of schooling[1] below the OECD average.
- For all subjects, student proficiency levels have improved steadily since 2006. Still, half of the students do not meet the basic proficiency level in Reading, Science and Math.

What may be driving student performance?

- **Socioeconomic background:** The performance gap between students at the top and bottom income quintiles has increased from 2 to 3 years of schooling since 2015.
- **Gender Gap:** Qatar has the largest gender gap in favor of girls of all PISA participating countries. The Reading performance gap has widened from 1.5 to over 2 years of schooling just since 2015.
- **School profile:** Students in private schools perform over 2.5 school years ahead of their public school counterparts.
- **Preschool:** Students with more than one year of preschool perform 1 year of schooling ahead of those with no preschool education.
- **School & Classroom:** Students in the top 40 percent of the Sense of Belonging Index[2] are close to 2 school years ahead of those in the bottom 40 percent. For the Disciplinary Climate Index[2], the difference between the top and bottom 40 percent is slightly over 2 school years.
- **Teachers:** Students in the top 40 percent of the Reading Stimulation Index are nearly 2 years of schooling ahead of those in the bottom 40 percent, implying a large effect of teacher practices on reading performance.

[1] 30 points in PISA scale ≈ 1 year of schooling
Note: Unless specified, student performance in the Takeaways Section refers to Reading scores.

SCORES OVER TIME

	MATHE-MATICS	READING	SCIENCE
2006	318	312	349
2009	368	372	379
2012	376	388	384
2015	402	402	418
2018	**414***	**407***	**419***

*Average 3-year trend is positive and statistically significant

Note: The average 3-year trend is the average change, per 3-year period, between the earliest available measurement in PISA and PISA 2018, calculated by a linear regression.

READING TRENDS

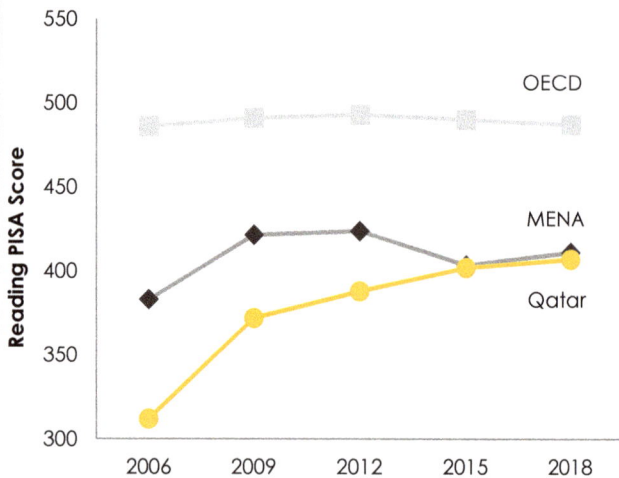

Middle East & North Africa

QATAR
PISA 2018

STUDENT PERFORMANCE

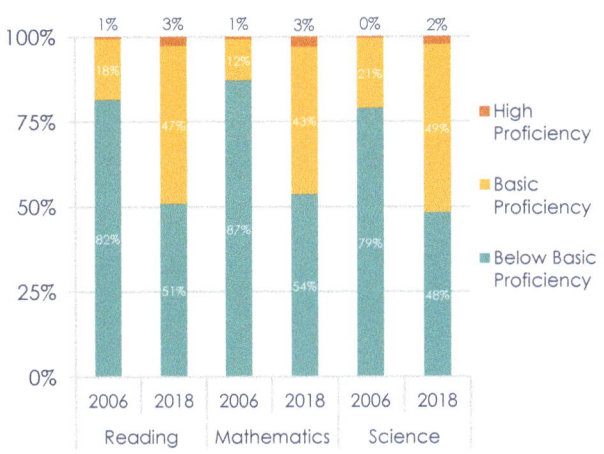

Functionally illiterate and innumerate students are those who do not meet the basic proficiency levels.

EQUITY PROFILE

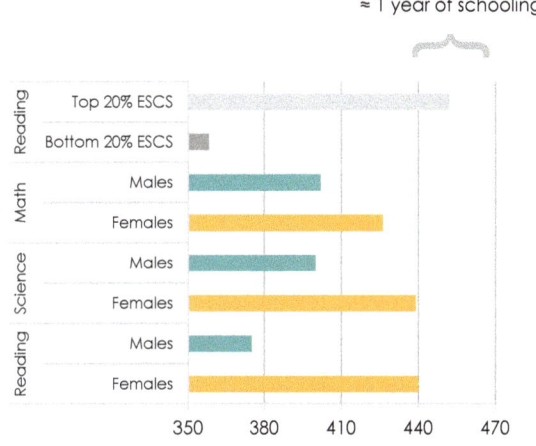

ESCS: Economic, Social and Cultural Status

SCHOOL PROFILE & PRESCHOOL

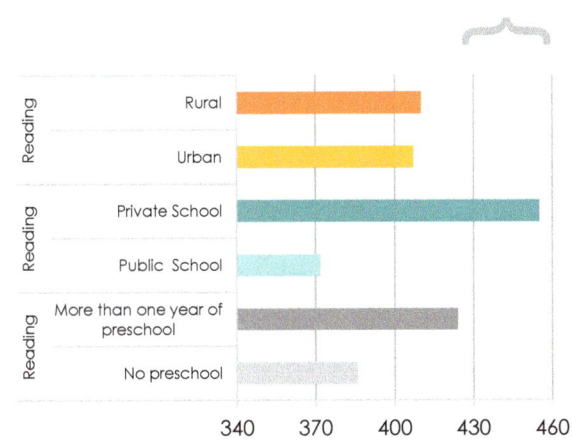

SCHOOL, CLASSROOM & TEACHER

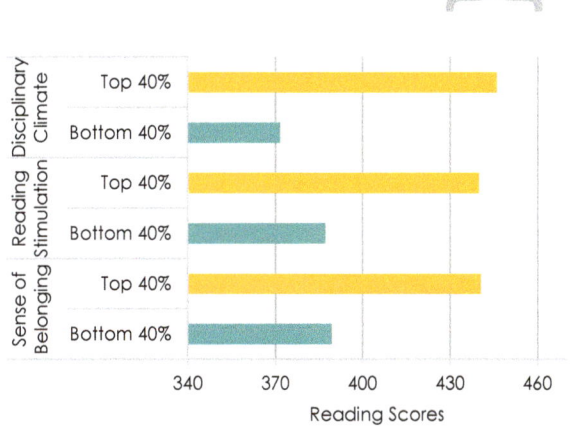

Reading Scores

[2] **Key to Indices:**
Disciplinary Climate Index measures the extent of classroom disruptions due to noise, disorder and other factors. **Reading Stimulation** is an index that measures teachers' stimulation of students' reading engagement. **Sense of Belonging** Index measures the extent to which students feel they belong to their school, make friends easily at school, etc. Top and Bottom 20% indicate percentiles in the corresponding indices.

Middle East & North Africa

QATAR
PISA 2018

PISA PERFORMANCE & GDP PER CAPITA

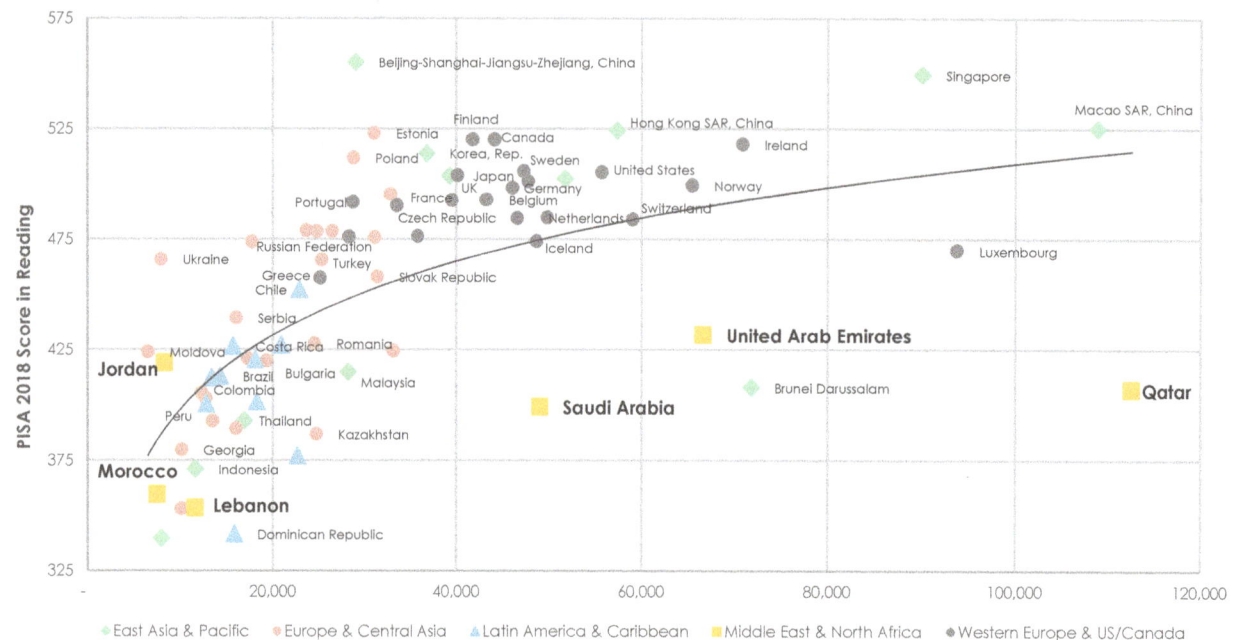

GDP per Capita 2018 (or latest), PPP (constant 2011 International $), World Bank ICP

WB EDUCATION ENGAGEMENT

No active World Bank education engagements as of December 2019.

ABOUT PISA

PISA: Programme for International Student Assessment

PISA is the OECD's benchmarking tool to assess achievement and application of key knowledge and skills of 15 year-olds. PISA tests proficiency in mathematics, reading, science, and problem-solving. It was launched in 2000 and is conducted every three years, with a focus on one of the subjects in each round. In 2018, the focus is on Reading. The test was taken by representative samples from 79 countries, including nearly 600,000 students. Six MENA countries participated in this PISA round: Jordan, Lebanon, Morocco, Qatar, Saudi Arabia and the United Arab Emirates. Functionally illiterate and innumerate students are those who do not meet the basic proficiency levels in reading, mathematics or science.

Note: For further information and implications for analyses of PISA data, please consult the PISA 2018 international report. *Source:* OECD, 2019. PISA 2018 Results (Volume 1): What Students Know and Can Do. Paris: OECD.

SAUDI ARABIA

Saudi Arabia

Human Capital Index Rank 73 out of 157

THE HUMAN CAPITAL INDEX (HCI) AND ITS COMPONENTS

The HCI measures the amount of human capital that a child born today can expect to attain by age 18. It conveys the productivity of the next generation of workers compared to a benchmark of complete education and full health. It is constructed for 157 countries.

It is made up of five indicators: the probability of survival to age five, a child's expected years of schooling, harmonized test scores as a measure of quality of learning, adult survival rate (fraction of 15-year olds that will survive to age 60), and the proportion of children who are not stunted.

Globally, 56 percent of all children born today will grow up to be, at best, half as productive as they could be; and 92 percent will grow up to be, at best, 75 percent as productive as they could be.

WHAT IS THE STATE OF HUMAN CAPITAL IN SAUDI ARABIA?

- **Human Capital Index.** A child born in Saudi Arabia today will be **58 percent** as productive when she grows up as she could be if she enjoyed complete education and full health.
- **Probability of Survival to Age 5.** 99 out of 100 children born in Saudi Arabia survive to age 5.
- **Expected Years of School.** In Saudi Arabia, a child who starts school at age 4 can expect to complete **12.4 years** of school by her 18th birthday.
- **Harmonized Test Scores.** Students in Saudi Arabia score **407** on a scale where 625 represents advanced attainment and 300 represents minimum attainment.
- **Learning-adjusted Years of School.** Factoring in what children actually learn, expected years of school is only **8.1 years**.
- **Adult Survival Rate.** Across Saudi Arabia, **91 percent** of 15-year olds will survive until age 60. This statistic is a proxy for the range of fatal and non-fatal health outcomes that a child born today would experience as an adult under current conditions.
- **Healthy Growth (Not Stunted Rate).** Data on stunting are not available for Saudi Arabia.

ARE THERE GENDER DIFFERENCES IN HCI?

In Saudi Arabia, the HCI for girls is higher than for boys. Table 1 shows gender disaggregation for each of the HCI components.

Figure 1. HCI and Components

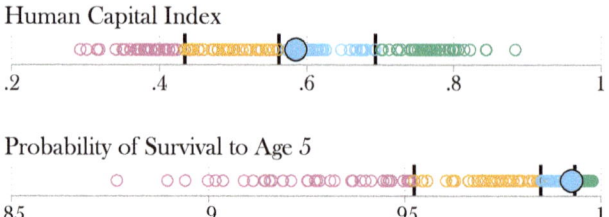
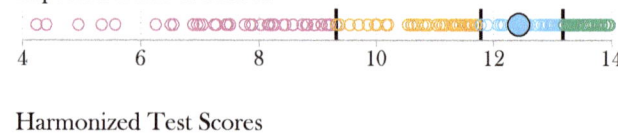

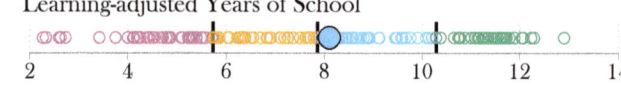

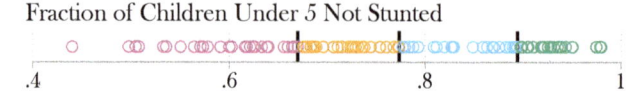

Note:
- Large circle represents Saudi Arabia
- Small circles represent other countries
- Thick, vertical lines and color of circles reflect quartiles of the distribution

Table 1. HCI by Gender

Component	Boys	Girls	Overall
HCI	0.56	0.61	0.58
Survival to Age 5	0.99	0.99	0.99
Expected Years of School	12.6	12.3	12.4
Harmonized Test Scores	380	436	407
Learning-adjusted Years of School	7.7	8.6	8.1
Adult Survival Rate	0.9	0.92	0.91
Not Stunted Rate	-	-	-

Note:
- When shown, hyphen denotes data are unavailable
- All values are rounded
- The gender-disaggregated HCI is calculated using only adult survival rates if gender-disaggregated stunting data is not available

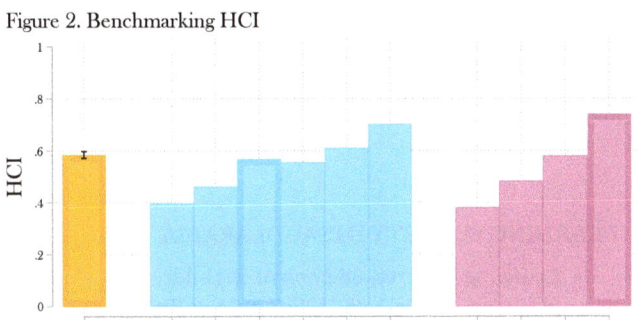

Figure 2. Benchmarking HCI

Notes:
- Unless specified all data are for 2017
- The uncertainty intervals (black vertical lines) reflect uncertainty in the measurement of components of the Index

HOW DOES SAUDI ARABIA COMPARE?

In 2017, Saudi Arabia's HCI is higher than the average for its region but lower than the average for its income group.

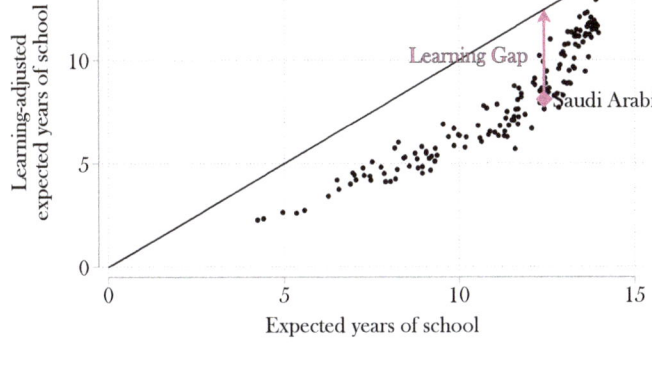

Figure 3. Learning Gap

HOW MUCH ARE CHILDREN ACTUALLY LEARNING IN SCHOOL?

Children in Saudi Arabia can expect to complete **12.4 years** of pre-primary, primary and secondary school by age 18. However, when years of schooling are adjusted for quality of learning, this is only equivalent to **8.1 years**: a learning gap of **4.3 years** (Figure 3).

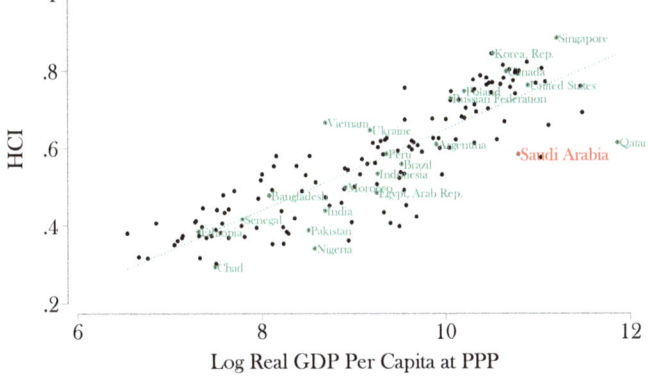

Figure 4. Human Capital Index vs GDP Per Capita

IS SAUDI ARABIA'S HCI IN LINE WITH WHAT IS PREDICTED FOR ITS INCOME LEVEL?

In 2017, the HCI for Saudi Arabia is lower than what would be predicted for its income level (Figure 4).

THE HUMAN CAPITAL PROJECT

The Human Capital Project seeks to raise awareness and increase demand for interventions to build human capital. It aims to accelerate better and more investments in people. The Project has three elements (i) the Human Capital Index, (ii) a program to strengthen research and measurement on human capital; and (iii) support to countries to accelerate progress in raising human capital outcomes.

For more information on the Human Capital Project please visit **www.worldbank.org/humancapitalproject**

 #**invest**inPeople

Saudi Arabia
Learning Poverty Brief

October 2019

AN EARLY-WARNING INDICATOR FOR THE HUMAN CAPITAL PROJECT

The Human Capital Project seeks to raise awareness and increase demand for interventions to build human capital. It aims to accelerate better and more investments in people.

In low- and middle-income countries, the learning crisis means that deficits in education outcomes are a major contributor to human capital deficits. Shortcomings in both the quantity of schooling and especially its quality explain a large part of the distance to the frontier. Addressing these shortcomings will require a multisectoral approach.

For more information on the Human Capital Project, please visit **www.worldbank.org/humancapitalproject**

WHY MEASURE LEARNING POVERTY?

All children should be able to read by age 10. As a major contributor to human capital deficits, the learning crisis undermines sustainable growth and poverty reduction. This brief summarizes some of the critical aspects of a new synthetic indicator, **Learning Poverty**, designed to help spotlight and galvanize action to address this crisis.

Eliminating Learning Poverty is as urgent as eliminating extreme monetary poverty, stunting, or hunger. The new data show that more than half of all children in low and middle-income countries suffer from Learning Poverty.

WHAT IS LEARNING POVERTY?

Learning Poverty means being unable to read and understand a short, age-appropriate text by age 10. All foundational skills are important, but we focus on reading because: (i) reading proficiency is an easily understood measure of learning; (ii) reading is a student's gateway to learning in every other area; and, (iii) reading proficiency can serve as a proxy for foundational learning in other subjects, in the same way that the absence of child stunting is a marker of healthy early childhood development.

HOW IS LEARNING POVERTY MEASURED?

This indicator brings together schooling and learning. It starts with the share of children who haven't achieved minimum reading proficiency and adjusts it by the proportion of children who are out of school.

$$LP = [BMP \times (1 - OoS)] + [1 \times OoS]$$

where, LP is Learning Poverty; BMP is share of children in school below minimum proficiency; OoS is the Percentage of Out-of-School children; and, in the case of OoS we assume $BMP = 1$.

The data used to calculate Learning Poverty has been made possible thanks to the work of the Global Alliance to Monitor Learning led by the UNESCO Institute for Statistics (UIS), which established Minimum Proficiency Levels (MPLs) that enable countries to benchmark learning across different cross-national and national assessments.

LEARNING POVERTY IN SAUDI ARABIA

- **Learning Poverty.** 38 percent of children in Saudi Arabia at late primary age today are not proficient in reading, adjusted for the Out-of-School children.
- **Out-of-School.** In Saudi Arabia, 3 percent of primary school-aged children are not enrolled in school. These children are excluded from learning in school.
- **Below Minimum Proficiency.** Large-scale learning assessments of students in Saudi Arabia indicate that 37 percent do not achieve the MPL at the end of primary school, proxied by data from grade 4 in 2016.

For countries with a very low Out-of-School population, the share of children Below Minimum Proficiency will be very close to the reported Learning Poverty.

Notes: The LP number for Saudi Arabia is calculated using the Global Learning Assessment Database (GLAD) harmonization based on PIRLS and the MPL threshold used was level Low (400 points). For more details, please consult the GLAD and Learning Poverty repositories in GitHub.

BENCHMARKING SAUDI ARABIA'S LEARNING POVERTY

Learning Poverty in Saudi Arabia is **25 percentage points better than** the average for the Middle East and North Africa region and **14.4 percentage points worse than** the average for high income countries.

Figure 1. Learning Poverty and components

Source: UIS and World Bank as of October 2019.

Notes: (1) Large circle represents Saudi Arabia; (2) Small circles represent other countries; and, (3) Vertical lines reflect the averages of Saudi Arabia's region and income group.

Saudi Arabia
Learning Poverty Brief

October 2019

HOW DOES SAUDI ARABIA'S GENDER GAP COMPARE GLOBALLY?

In Saudi Arabia, lack of data prevents comparisons of Learning Poverty for boys and girls.

Table 1 shows sex disaggregation for Learning Poverty and HCI education components whenever available.

Table 1. Sex Disaggregation

Indicators and Components	Boys	Girls	All
Learning Poverty	NA	NA	38.3
Below Minimum Proficiency	49.4	23	36.7
Out-of-School	NA	NA	2.5
Human Capital Index	0.56	0.61	0.58
Learning-adjusted Years of Schooling	7.7	8.6	8.1

Source: UIS and World Bank for LP, BMP and OoS as of October 2019; EdStats/WDI for HCI and LAYS; The Full Learning Poverty database is available for download at the Development Data Hub.

Figure 2. Gender Gap - Learning Poverty by Sex

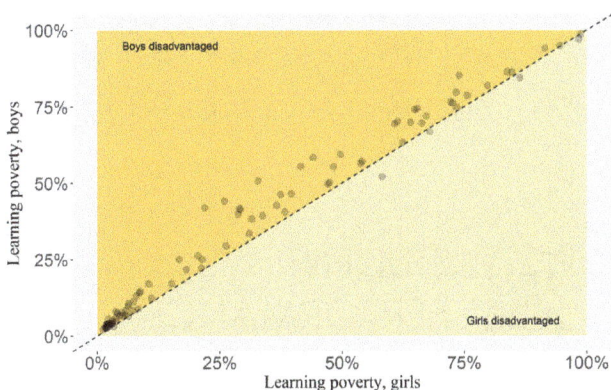

Source: UIS and World Bank as of October 2019. *Notes:* (1) No gender split in Learning Poverty is available for Saudi Arabia. Only countries with data displayed; and, (2) The closer a country is to the dotted line the smaller its LP gender gap.

POINT OF CONTACT

Saudi Arabia: Laura Gregory

Middle East and North Africa: Laura Gregory

PRIMARY EDUCATION EXPENDITURE

Primary education expenditure per child of primary education age in Saudi Arabia is **USD 8,627 (PPP)**, which is **55.5% above** the average for the Middle East and North Africa region and **2.6% above** the average for high income countries.

Figure 3. Expenditure per child in primary school age

Source: UIS and World Bank as of October 2019. *Note:* Primary education expenditure per child is calculated as total expenditure on primary education divided by total number of children of primary school age. Data for Saudi Arabia is from 2007.

DATA AND DATA GAPS ON LEARNING AND SCHOOLING IN SAUDI ARABIA

Saudi Arabia administer a National Large-Scale Assessment (NLSA) at the End of Primary school, according to UIS SDG 4.1.2b monitoring. Once this NLSA is mapped against UIS/SDG4.1.1 reporting standards it should be possible to monitor Learning Poverty with it.

Saudi Arabia participated in the following published cross-national learning assessments in recent years: TIMSS (2003, 2007, 2011, 2015) and PIRLS (2011, 2016).

Saudi Arabia has not participated in the World Bank's LeAP diagnostic exercise to analyze its assessment system. To get started, contact the LeAP team.

The Out-of-School adjustment in our Learning Poverty indicator relies on enrollment data. Our preferred definition is the adjusted net primary enrollment as reported by UIS. This data relies both on the population Census and the EMIS. In the case of Saudi Arabia, the preferred definition based on the EMIS data is for 2014.

Notes: The definition of NLSA does not include National Exams; LeAP: Learning Assessment Platform (LeAP-team@worldbank.org). TIMSS: Trends in International Mathematics and Science Study. PIRLS: Progress in International Reading Literacy Study.

 #investinPeople

Disclaimer: The numbers presented in this brief are based on global data harmonization efforts conducted by UIS and the World Bank that increase cross-country comparability of selected findings from official statistics. For that reason, the numbers discussed here may be different from official statistics reported by governments and national offices of statistics. Such differences are due to the different purposes of the statistics, which can be for global comparison or to meet national definitions.

#INVESTinPeople

Middle East & North Africa

SAUDI ARABIA
PISA 2018

 TAKEAWAYS

A first-time PISA participant, Saudi Arabia scored poorly in all three subjects.

- Student performance is lower than in Qatar and UAE, below the MENA average, and between 3 or 4 years of schooling[1] below the OECD average, depending on the subject.
- In all three subjects, at least half the students do not meet the basic proficiency level (Reading), and up to a substantial 73 percent in Math.

What may be driving poor performance?

- **Socioeconomic background:** There are differences equivalent to 2 years of schooling between the performance of students in the top and bottom income quintiles.

- **Gender gap:** Girls outperform boys in all three subjects, with the largest gap occurring in Reading (equivalent to 2 years of schooling and one of the largest of all PISA countries).

- **School profile and location:** The performance of students in private schools is nearly 1 school year ahead of those in public schools, while differences of 1 school year exist between students in urban and rural schools.

- **School & classroom:** Students in the top 40 percent of the Sense of Belonging Index[2] are more than 1 year of schooling ahead of those in the bottom 40 percent. Closely related is the Disciplinary Climate Index[2], where students in the top 40 percent are over 1 school year ahead of those in the bottom 40 percent.

- **Teachers:** Students in the top 40 percent of the Stimulation to Read Index[2] score 1 school year ahead of those in the bottom 40 percent. This points to a significant impact of teaching practices on student performance in Reading.

[1] 30 points in PISA scale ≈ 1 year of schooling
Note: Unless specified, student performance in the *Takeaways* Section refers to Science scores.

 SCORES PISA 2018

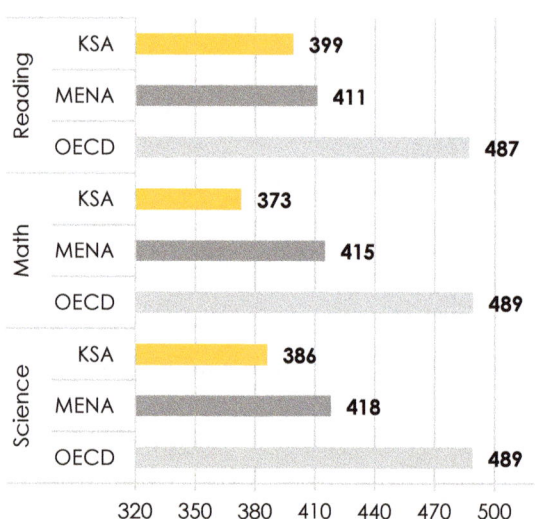

 STUDENT PERFORMANCE

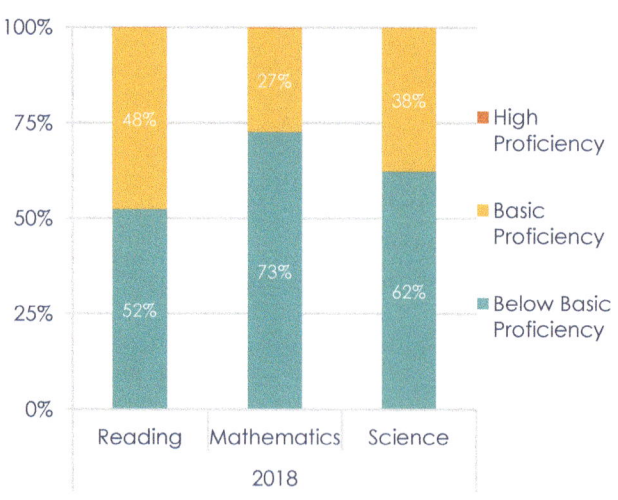

Functionally illiterate and innumerate students are those who do not meet the basic proficiency levels.

Middle East & North Africa

SAUDI ARABIA
PISA 2018

SCHOOL PROFILE & PRESCHOOL

EQUITY PROFILE

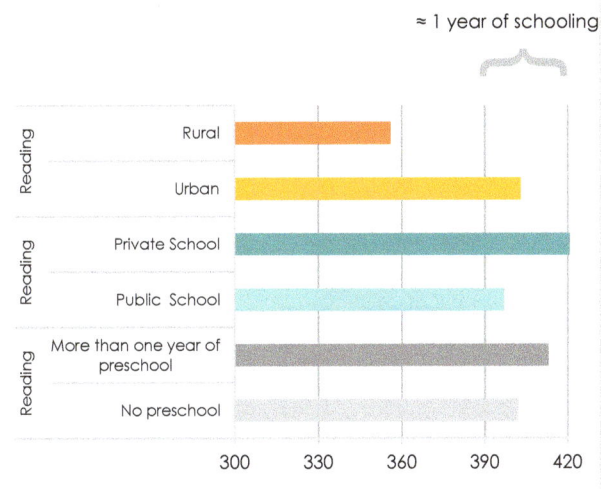

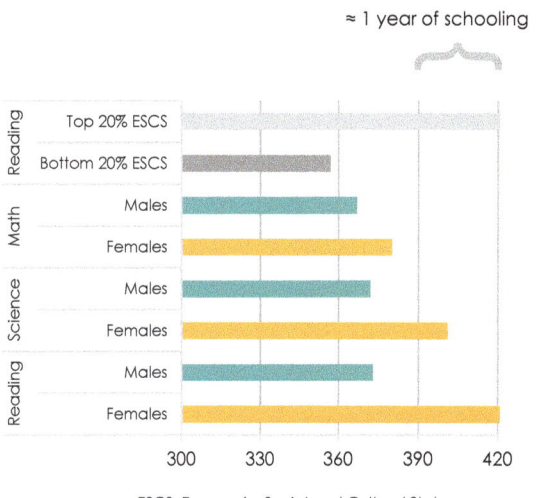

ESCS: Economic, Social and Cultural Status

SCHOOL, CLASSROOM & TEACHER

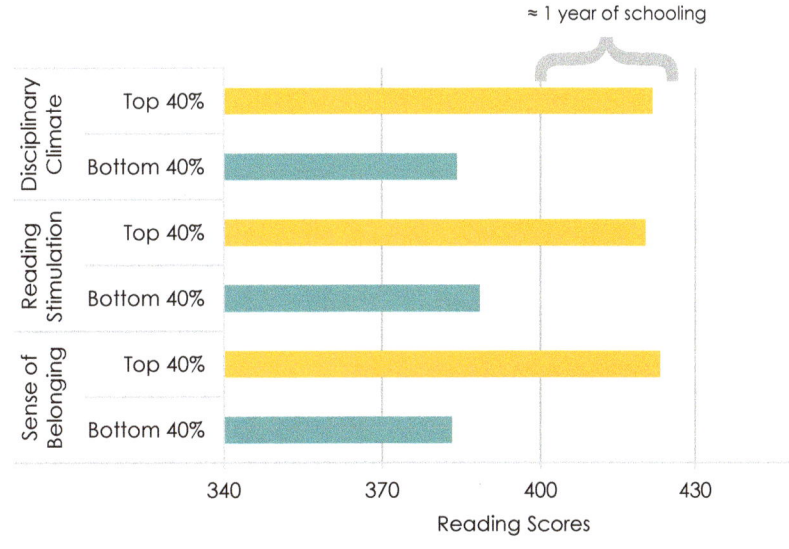

[2] **Key to Indices:**
Disciplinary Climate Index measures the extent of classroom disruptions due to noise, disorder and other factors. **Reading Stimulation** is an index that measures teachers' stimulation of students' reading engagement. **Sense of Belonging** Index measures the extent to which students feel they belong to their school, make friends easily at school, etc. Top and Bottom 20% indicate percentiles in the corresponding indices.

100 | FOSTERING HUMAN CAPITAL IN THE GULF COOPERATION COUNCIL COUNTRIES

Middle East & North Africa

SAUDI ARABIA
PISA 2018

 **PISA PERFORMANCE & GDP PER CAPITA**

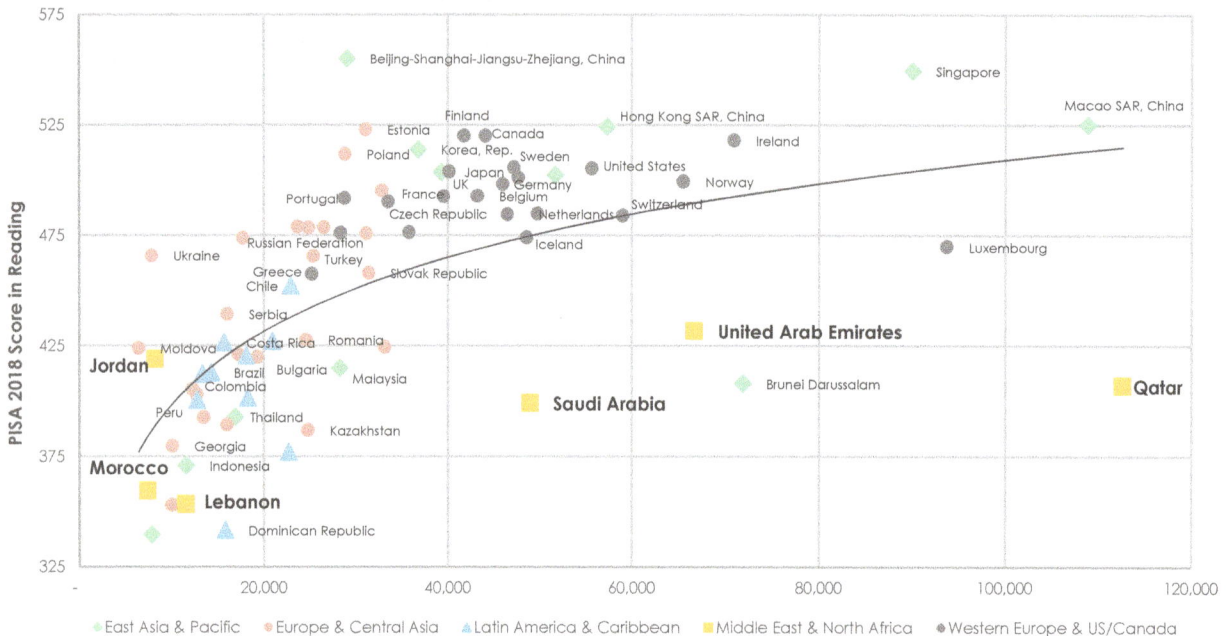

GDP per Capita 2018 (or latest), PPP (constant 2011 International $), World Bank ICP

WB EDUCATION ENGAGEMENT

REIMBURSABLE ADVISORY SERVICES

- *Supporting Quality Education in Saudi Arabia* with the Ministry of Education
- *Education Sector Program Phase 2* with the Education and Training Evaluation Commission.

ABOUT PISA

PISA: Program for International Student Assessment

PISA is the OECD's benchmarking tool to assess achievement and application of key knowledge and skills of 15 year-olds. PISA tests proficiency in mathematics, reading, science, and problem-solving. It was launched in 2000 and is conducted every three years, with a focus on one of the subjects in each round. In 2018, the focus is on Reading. The test was taken by representative samples from 79 countries, including nearly 600,000 students. Six MENA countries participated in this PISA round: Jordan, Lebanon, Morocco, Qatar, Saudi Arabia and the United Arab Emirates. Functionally illiterate and innumerate students are those who do not meet the basic proficiency levels in reading, mathematics or science.

Note: For further information and implications for analyses of PISA data, please consult the PISA 2018 international report. *Source:* OECD, 2019. *PISA 2018 Results (Volume 1): What Students Know and Can Do.* Paris: OECD.

UNITED ARAB EMIRATES

United Arab Emirates
Human Capital Index Rank 49 out of 157

THE HUMAN CAPITAL INDEX (HCI) AND ITS COMPONENTS

The HCI measures the amount of human capital that a child born today can expect to attain by age 18. It conveys the productivity of the next generation of workers compared to a benchmark of complete education and full health. It is constructed for 157 countries.

It is made up of five indicators: the probability of survival to age five, a child's expected years of schooling, harmonized test scores as a measure of quality of learning, adult survival rate (fraction of 15-year olds that will survive to age 60), and the proportion of children who are not stunted.

Globally, 56 percent of all children born today will grow up to be, at best, half as productive as they could be; and 92 percent will grow up to be, at best, 75 percent as productive as they could be.

WHAT IS THE STATE OF HUMAN CAPITAL IN THE UNITED ARAB EMIRATES?

- **Human Capital Index.** A child born in the United Arab Emirates today will be **66 percent** as productive when she grows up as she could be if she enjoyed complete education and full health.
- **Probability of Survival to Age 5.** **99** out of 100 children born in the United Arab Emirates survive to age 5.
- **Expected Years of School.** In the United Arab Emirates, a child who starts school at age 4 can expect to complete **13.1 years** of school by her 18th birthday.
- **Harmonized Test Scores.** Students in the United Arab Emirates score **451** on a scale where 625 represents advanced attainment and 300 represents minimum attainment.
- **Learning-adjusted Years of School.** Factoring in what children actually learn, expected years of school is only **9.5 years**.
- **Adult Survival Rate.** Across the United Arab Emirates, **93 percent** of 15-year olds will survive until age 60. This statistic is a proxy for the range of fatal and non-fatal health outcomes that a child born today would experience as an adult under current conditions.
- **Healthy Growth (Not Stunted Rate).** Data on stunting are not available for the United Arab Emirates.

ARE THERE GENDER DIFFERENCES IN HCI?

In the United Arab Emirates, lack of data prevents comparison of HCI by gender. Table 1 shows gender disaggregation for each of the HCI components, where available.

Figure 1. HCI and Components

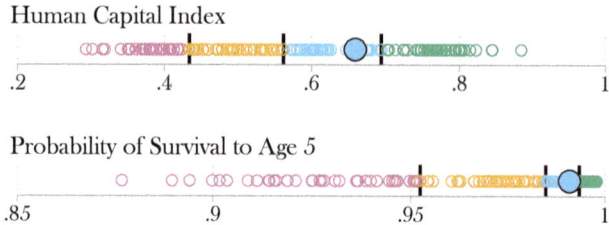
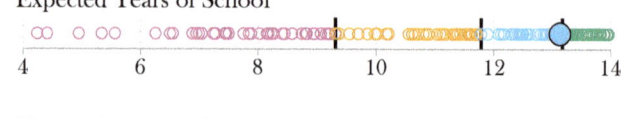
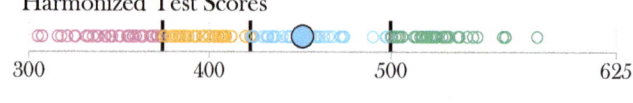
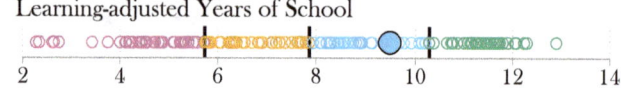

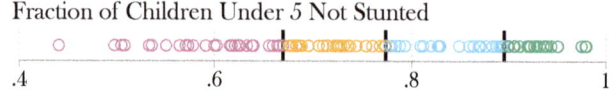

Note:
- Large circle represents United Arab Emirates
- Small circles represent other countries
- Thick, vertical lines and color of circles reflect quartiles of the distribution

Table 1. HCI by Gender

Component	Boys	Girls	Overall
HCI	-	-	0.66
Survival to Age 5	0.99	0.99	0.99
Expected Years of School	-	-	13.1
Harmonized Test Scores	439	464	451
Learning-adjusted Years of School	-	-	9.5
Adult Survival Rate	0.92	0.95	0.93
Not Stunted Rate	-	-	-

Note:
- When shown, hyphen denotes data are unavailable
- All values are rounded
- The gender-disaggregated HCI is calculated using only adult survival rates if gender-disaggregated stunting data is not available

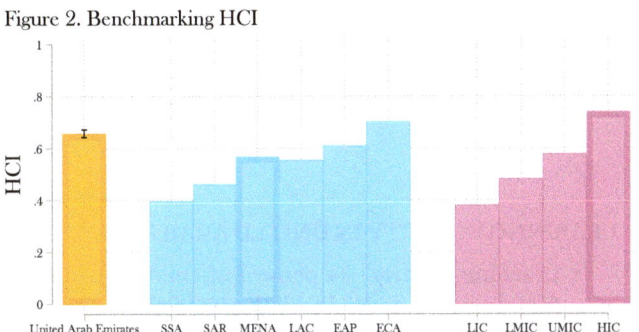

Figure 2. Benchmarking HCI

Notes:
- Unless specified all data are for 2017
- The uncertainty intervals (black vertical lines) reflect uncertainty in the measurement of components of the Index

HOW DOES THE UNITED ARAB EMIRATES COMPARE?

In 2017, the United Arab Emirates' HCI is higher than the average for its region but lower than the average for its income group.

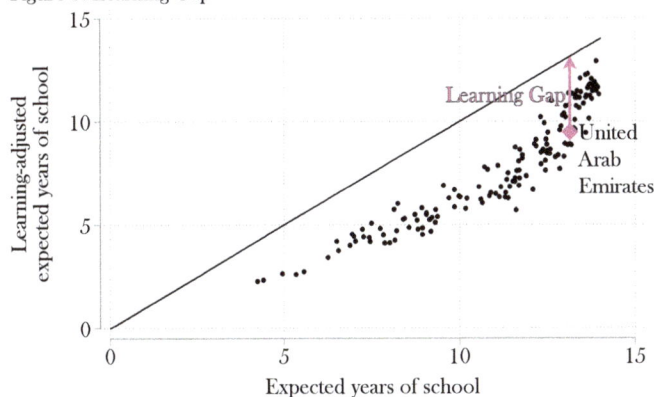

Figure 3. Learning Gap

HOW MUCH ARE CHILDREN ACTUALLY LEARNING IN SCHOOL?

Children in the United Arab Emirates can expect to complete **13.1 years** of pre-primary, primary and secondary school by age 18. However, when years of schooling are adjusted for quality of learning, this is only equivalent to **9.5 years**: a learning gap of **3.6 years** (Figure 3).

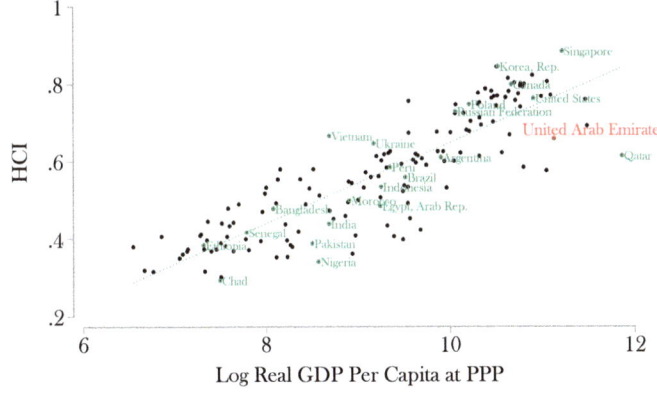

Figure 4. Human Capital Index vs GDP Per Capita

IS THE UNITED ARAB EMIRATES' HCI IN LINE WITH WHAT IS PREDICTED FOR ITS INCOME LEVEL?

In 2017, the HCI for the United Arab Emirates is lower than what would be predicted for its income level (Figure 4).

THE HUMAN CAPITAL PROJECT

The Human Capital Project seeks to raise awareness and increase demand for interventions to build human capital. It aims to accelerate better and more investments in people. The Project has three elements (i) the Human Capital Index, (ii) a program to strengthen research and measurement on human capital; and (iii) support to countries to accelerate progress in raising human capital outcomes.

For more information on the Human Capital Project please visit **www.worldbank.org/humancapitalproject**

 #**invest**inPeople

United Arab Emirates
Learning Poverty Brief

October 2019

AN EARLY-WARNING INDICATOR FOR THE HUMAN CAPITAL PROJECT

The Human Capital Project seeks to raise awareness and increase demand for interventions to build human capital. It aims to accelerate better and more investments in people.

In low- and middle-income countries, the learning crisis means that deficits in education outcomes are a major contributor to human capital deficits. Shortcomings in both the quantity of schooling and especially its quality explain a large part of the distance to the frontier. Addressing these shortcomings will require a multisectoral approach.

For more information on the Human Capital Project, please visit **www.worldbank.org/humancapitalproject**

WHY MEASURE LEARNING POVERTY?

All children should be able to read by age 10. As a major contributor to human capital deficits, the learning crisis undermines sustainable growth and poverty reduction. This brief summarizes some of the critical aspects of a new synthetic indicator, **Learning Poverty**, designed to help spotlight and galvanize action to address this crisis.

Eliminating Learning Poverty is as urgent as eliminating extreme monetary poverty, stunting, or hunger. The new data show that more than half of all children in low and middle-income countries suffer from Learning Poverty.

WHAT IS LEARNING POVERTY?

Learning Poverty means being unable to read and understand a short, age-appropriate text by age 10. All foundational skills are important, but we focus on reading because: (i) reading proficiency is an easily understood measure of learning; (ii) reading is a student's gateway to learning in every other area; and, (iii) reading proficiency can serve as a proxy for foundational learning in other subjects, in the same way that the absence of child stunting is a marker of healthy early childhood development.

HOW IS LEARNING POVERTY MEASURED?

This indicator brings together schooling and learning. It starts with the share of children who haven't achieved minimum reading proficiency and adjusts it by the proportion of children who are out of school.

$$LP = [BMP \times (1 - OoS)] + [1 \times OoS]$$

where, LP is Learning Poverty; BMP is share of children in school below minimum proficiency; OoS is the Percentage of Out-of-School children; and, in the case of OoS we assume $BMP = 1$.

The data used to calculate Learning Poverty has been made possible thanks to the work of the Global Alliance to Monitor Learning led by the UNESCO Institute for Statistics (UIS), which established Minimum Proficiency Levels (MPLs) that enable countries to benchmark learning across different cross-national and national assessments.

LEARNING POVERTY IN UNITED ARAB EMIRATES

- **Learning Poverty.** 34 percent of children in United Arab Emirates at late primary age today are not proficient in reading, adjusted for the Out-of-School children.
- **Out-of-School.** In United Arab Emirates, 3 percent of primary school-aged children are not enrolled in school. These children are excluded from learning in school.
- **Below Minimum Proficiency.** Large-scale learning assessments of students in United Arab Emirates indicate that 32 percent do not achieve the MPL at the end of primary school, proxied by data from grade 4 in 2016.

For countries with a very low Out-of-School population, the share of children Below Minimum Proficiency will be very close to the reported Learning Poverty.

Notes: The LP number for United Arab Emirates is calculated using the Global Learning Assessment Database (GLAD) harmonization based on PIRLS and the MPL threshold used was level Low (400 points). For more details, please consult the GLAD and Learning Poverty repositories in GitHub.

BENCHMARKING UNITED ARAB EMIRATES'S LEARNING POVERTY

Learning Poverty in United Arab Emirates is **29 percentage points better than** the average for the Middle East and North Africa region and **10.4 percentage points worse than** the average for high income countries.

Figure 1. Learning Poverty and components

Source: UIS and World Bank as of October 2019.

Notes: (1) Large circle represents United Arab Emirates; (2) Small circles represent other countries; and, (3) Vertical lines reflect the averages of United Arab Emirates's region and income group.

#INVESTinPeople

United Arab Emirates
Learning Poverty Brief

October 2019

HOW DOES UNITED ARAB EMIRATES'S GENDER GAP COMPARE GLOBALLY?

As in most countries, **Learning Poverty is higher for boys than for girls** in United Arab Emirates.

This result is a composition of two effects. First the share of **Out-of-School children is lower for boys** (2%) than for girls (3.6%).

And second **boys are less likely to achieve minimum proficiency** at the end of primary school (38.5%) than girls (26%) in United Arab Emirates.

Table 1 shows sex disaggregation for Learning Poverty and HCI education components whenever available.

Table 1. Sex Disaggregation

Indicators and Components	Boys	Girls	All
Learning Poverty	39.7	28.7	34.3
Below Minimum Proficiency	38.5	26	32.4
Out-of-School	2	3.6	2.8
Human Capital Index	NA	NA	0.66
Learning-adjusted Years of Schooling	NA	NA	9.5

Source: UIS and World Bank for LP, BMP and OoS as of October 2019; EdStats/WDI for HCI and LAYS; The Full Learning Poverty database is available for download at the Development Data Hub.

Figure 2. Gender Gap - Learning Poverty by Sex

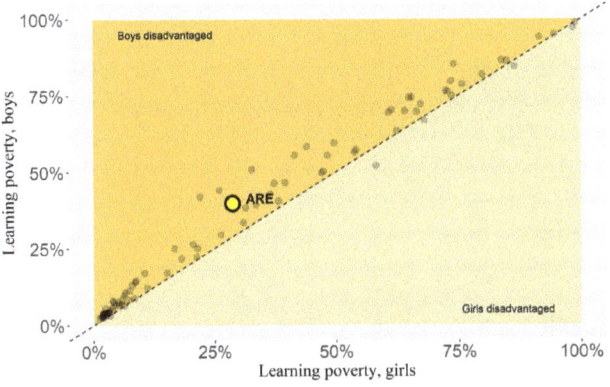

Source: UIS and World Bank as of October 2019. *Notes:* (1) - Large circle represents United Arab Emirates; and, (2) The closer a country is to the dotted line the smaller its LP gender gap.

POINT OF CONTACT

United Arab Emirates: Igor Kheyftes
Middle East and North Africa: Laura Gregory

PRIMARY EDUCATION EXPENDITURE

Primary education expenditure per child of primary education age in United Arab Emirates is **USD 5,891 (PPP)**, which is **6.2% above** the average for the Middle East and North Africa region and **30% below** the average for high income countries.

Figure 3. Expenditure per child in primary school age

Source: UIS and World Bank as of October 2019. *Note:* Primary education expenditure per child is calculated as total expenditure on primary education divided by total number of children of primary school age. Data for United Arab Emirates is from 1998.

DATA AND DATA GAPS ON LEARNING AND SCHOOLING IN UNITED ARAB EMIRATES

United Arab Emirates administer a National Large-Scale Assessment (NLSA) at the End of Primary school, according to UIS SDG 4.1.2b monitoring. Once this NLSA is mapped against UIS/SDG4.1.1 reporting standards it should be possible to monitor Learning Poverty with it.

United Arab Emirates participated in the following published cross-national learning assessments in recent years: TIMSS (2011, 2015), PIRLS (2011, 2016) and PISA (2009, 2012, 2015).

According to the World Bank's 2013 LeAP diagnostic analysis of United Arab Emirates's assessment system, the country's ratings on large-scale assessment activities were **Established (3 out of 4)** on Cross-National Learning Assessment and **Established (3 out of 4)** on NLSA. To update results, contact the LeAP team.

The Out-of-School adjustment in our Learning Poverty indicator relies on enrollment data. Our preferred definition is the adjusted net primary enrollment as reported by UIS. This data relies both on the population Census and the EMIS. In the case of United Arab Emirates, the preferred definition based on the EMIS data is for 2016.

Notes: The definition of NLSA does not include National Exams; LeAP: Learning Assessment Platform (LeAP-team@worldbank.org). TIMSS: Trends in International Mathematics and Science Study. PIRLS: Progress in International Reading Literacy Study. PISA: Programme for International Student Assessment.

 #investinPeople

Disclaimer: The numbers presented in this brief are based on global data harmonization efforts conducted by UIS and the World Bank that increase cross-country comparability of selected findings from official statistics. For that reason, the numbers discussed here may be different from official statistics reported by governments and national offices of statistics. Such differences are due to the different purposes of the statistics, which can be for global comparison or to meet national definitions.

#INVESTinPeople

UNITED ARAB EMIRATES
PISA 2018

TAKEAWAYS

Student performance in the UAE continues to top the MENA region despite the fact that basic proficiency levels in all subjects have steadily declined since 2009

- The percentage of students still not achieving the basic proficiency level in Reading has increased to 43 percent, up from 31 in 2009.
- The increase of 8 points in Math marks the first time ever that UAE shows an increase in performance in any of the three subjects.

What may be driving student performance?

- **Socioeconomic background:** There are differences equivalent to nearly 3.5 years of schooling between the performance of students at the top and low income quintiles (up from 2 years back in 2015).
- **Gender Gap:** Girls outperform boys in all three subjects, with a gap equivalent to 2 school years in Reading (up from 1.5 back in 2015)
- **School type and location:** The performance of students in private schools is 2.5 school years ahead of their public school counterparts[1], while differences of one school year exist between students in urban and rural schools (down from 2 years in 2015).
- **School & Classroom:** Students in the top 40 percent of the Sense of Belonging Index[2] are around 1.5 years of schooling ahead of those in the bottom 40 percent. Closely related is the Disciplinary Climate Index[2], for which the difference in performance between the top and bottom quintiles rose to nearly 2.5 school years (up from 1 year in 2015).
- **Teachers:** Students in the top 40 percent of the Stimulation to Read Index[2] score the equivalent of 1.5 school years ahead of those in the bottom 40 percent. This points to a considerable impact of teaching practices on Reading student performance.

[1] 30 points in PISA scale ≈ 1 year of schooling
Note: Unless specified, student performance in the Takeaways Section refers to Science scores.

SCORES OVER TIME

	MATHE-MATICS	READING	SCIENCE
2009	421	431	438
2012	434	442	448
2015	427	434	437
2018	435+	432-	434-

+Average 3-year trend is positive but not statistically significant
-Average 3-year trend is negative but not statistically significant

Note: The average 3-year trend is the average change, per 3-year period, between the earliest available measurement in PISA and PISA 2018, calculated by a linear regression. 2009 PISA scores pertain to Dubai.

READING TRENDS

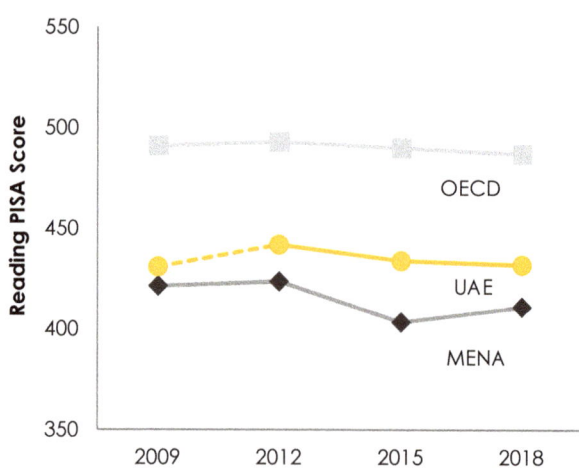

Note: 2009 PISA scores pertain to Dubai.

Middle East & North Africa

UNITED ARAB EMIRATES
PISA 2018

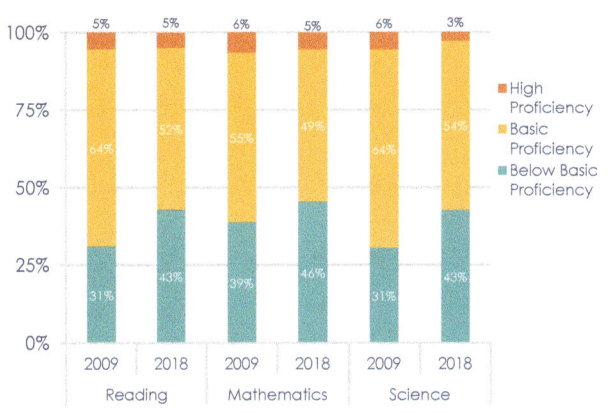

Note: Functionally illiterate and innumerate students are those who do not meet the basic proficiency levels. 2009 PISA scores pertain to Dubai.

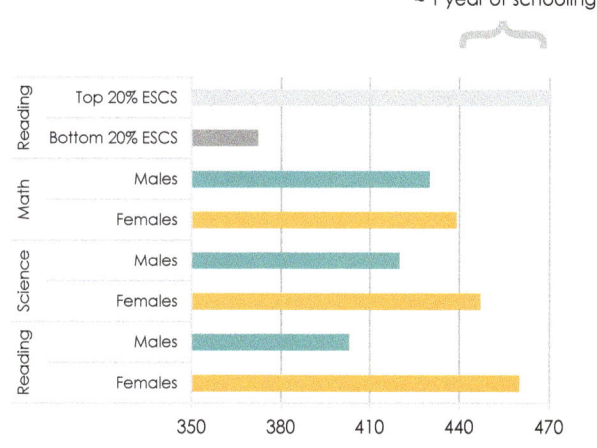

ESCS: Economic, Social and Cultural Status

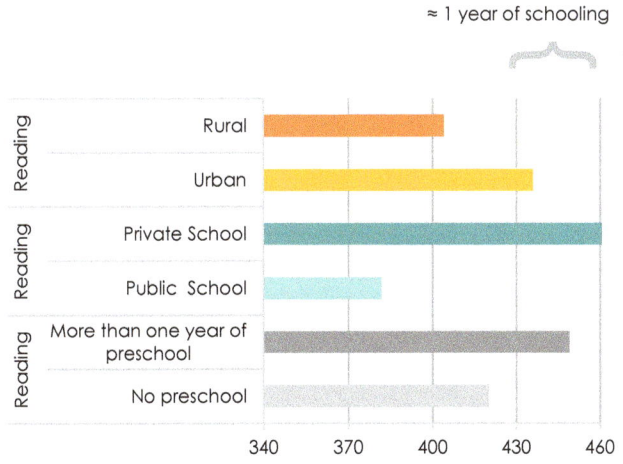

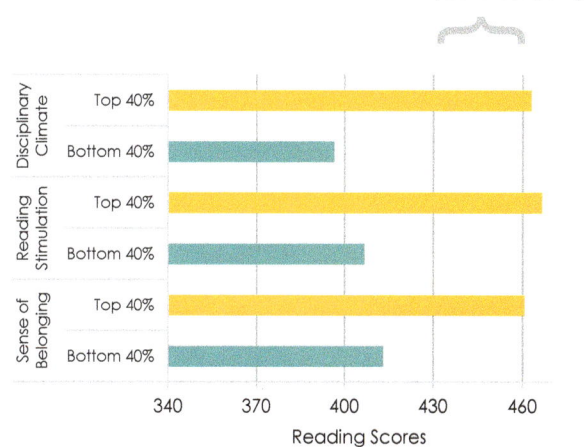

[2] Key to Indices:
Disciplinary Climate Index measures the extent of classroom disruptions due to noise, disorder and other factors. **Reading Stimulation** is an index that measures teachers' stimulation of students' reading engagement. **Sense of Belonging** Index measures the extent to which students feel they belong to their school, make friends easily at school, etc. Top and Bottom 20% indicate percentiles in the corresponding indices.

UNITED ARAB EMIRATES
PISA 2018

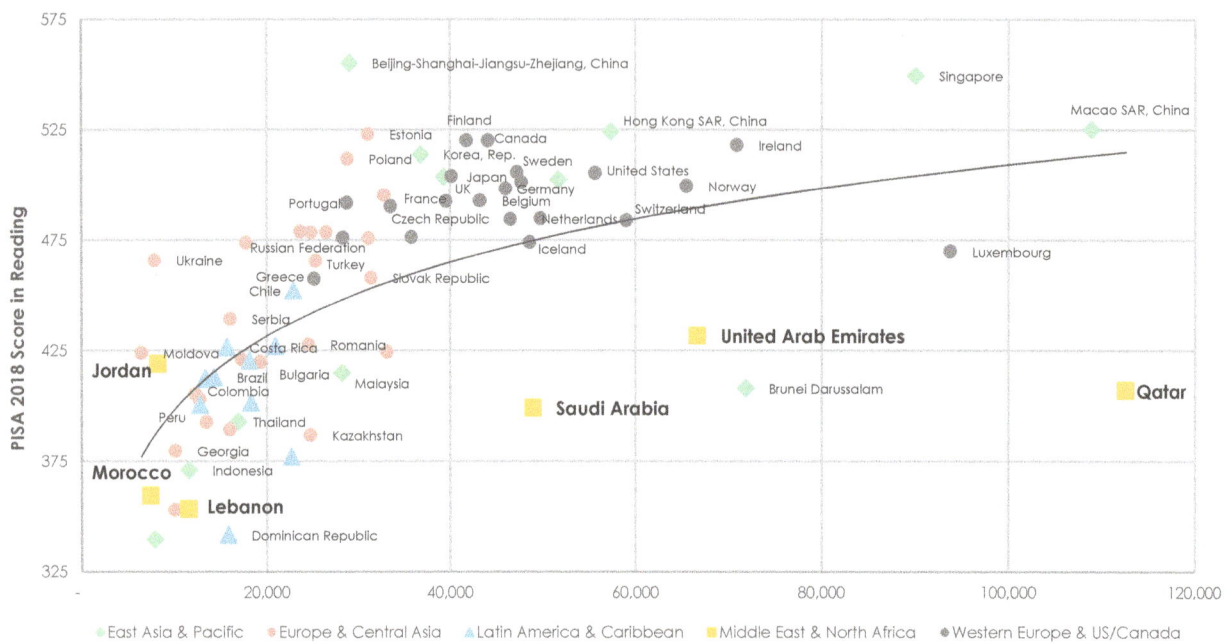

PISA PERFORMANCE & GDP PER CAPITA

GDP per Capita 2018 (or latest), PPP (constant 2011 International $), World Bank ICP

WB EDUCATION ENGAGEMENT

No active World Bank education engagements.

ABOUT PISA

PISA: Program for International Student Assessment

PISA is the OECD's benchmarking tool to assess achievement and application of key knowledge and skills of 15 year-olds. PISA tests proficiency in mathematics, reading, science, and problem-solving. It was launched in 2000 and is conducted every three years, with a focus on one of the subjects in each round. In 2018, the focus is on Reading. The test was taken by representative samples from 79 countries, including nearly 600,000 students. Six MENA countries participated in this PISA round: Jordan, Lebanon, Morocco, Qatar, Saudi Arabia and the United Arab Emirates. Functionally illiterate and innumerate students are those who do not meet the basic proficiency levels in reading, mathematics or science.

Note: For further information and implications for analyses of PISA data, please consult the PISA 2018 international report. *Source:* OECD, 2019. *PISA 2018 Results (Volume 1): What Students Know and Can Do.* Paris: OECD.

www.ingramcontent.com/pod-product-compliance
Ingram Content Group UK Ltd.
Pitfield, Milton Keynes, MK11 3LW, UK
UKHW050855220326
11408UKWH00007B/605